with the
Church of God

A Challenge to Ministry Leaders

J. Thomas Pelt

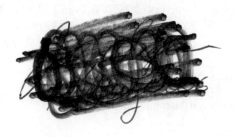

Warner Press

a subsidiary of Church of God Ministries, Inc.
ANDERSON, INDIANA

Coordinator of Communications and Publishing
Church of God Ministries, Inc.
PO Box 2420
Anderson, IN 46018-2420
800-848-2464
www.chog.org

To purchase additional copies of this book, to inquire about distribution and
for all other sales-related matters, please contact:

Warner Press, Inc.
PO Box 2499
Anderson, IN 46018-9988
877-346-3974
www.warnerpress.com

Cover design by Carolyn Kuchar
Text design by Joseph D. Allison
Edited by Stephen R. Lewis and Joseph D. Allison

ISBN-13: 978-1-59317-139-1
ISBN-10: 1-59317-139-0

Printed in the United States of America.
06 07 08 09 10 / EP/ 10 9 8 7 6 5 4 3 2 1

Dedication

To my father, Thomas Pelt...
my coach, pastor, mentor, and friend.

You have so faithfully shown me all that is right about the
Church of God. I love and honor you.

Contents

Preface

WHAT'S WRONG *with the Church of God?* That was my original title. Don't like the sound of it? Not very long into my first draft, it began to get to me, too. It has a negative, even defeatist connotation. After all, the mere assertion that there is something fundamentally wrong with our movement bothers all of us. However, my reasoning behind the original title of this work remains unchanged, that is: If we truly believe that the Church of God reformation movement has an ordained place in the greater Kingdom as we hasten to the second coming, and if we love the movement for this, then we must dare to ask such questions and dare to answer them proactively. However, I will try to look on the bright side throughout this book, keeping before us all that is truly right about the movement known as the Church of God. Sure, our last few decades have been less than memorable in some ways, but the embers of revival's fires are still glowing, just waiting for a wind to fan them into flame (2 Tim 1:6).

This book does not pretend to be a great theological or historical treatise concerning our movement. Nor do I pretend to be a writer in the line of the many great authors of our movement, past or present. I am a pastor, not a writer. This book is simply a cry of the heart for all who share a love for the Church of God. It is a dare, if you will—a dare to seek God's guidance as never before, a dare to begin that quest with a long, hard, introspective look in the mirror. I intend this book to be motivational and instigating, even provoking deliberate debate from a deep desire to grow rather than a somewhat resigned sense of, oh well, that's just the way things are. Some subjects may find their way into numerous chapters. I pray this does not belabor any point but only emphasizes its import. Hyperbole is employed from time to time. Some will say that its vision is a little pie-in-the-sky. So be it. Maybe this book will make a few people angry enough to prove its suppositions wrong, then actually attempt to do something about it. Oh, that we would all strive to grow some powerful local, regional, and state ministries that impact individuals, families, communities, and even cultures for Christ! If only we would put some move back into the movement by God's grace and for his glory!

On what authority do I suggest these things? On that revealed in the many Scripture passages I have referenced, along with some pastoral experience. My wife and I are both PKs (preacher's kids) in the Church of God and have a total of twelve ordained ministers throughout the branches of our family tree. In the past decade, I have had the joyous privilege of attending, chairing, singing, preaching, and teaching at local, state, and national camp meetings, conferences, conventions, think tanks, focus groups, and other assemblies of the Church of God. I have worked hand in hand and heart to heart with many of our most respected leaders. I am convinced that I have received far more than I have added to those groups and experiences. To be sure, I have taken page after page of notes as I have sat under the teaching of so many of our great leaders, some of whom are still with us and others whom have gone on to their reward. I share this brief pedigree, such as it is, only in the hope that you might see my experience in the Church of God as enough justification to continue reading.

Even now, I feel that I have not adequately expressed my heart for the Church of God or the heart cry I have heard from so many people over the past few years. I also worry that I may have overstated the case for change. Either way, I do not pretend to represent any particular group. Rather, I sense that I am part of an emerging spirit among many (some of whom have longed for it much longer than I) desiring that the Church of God reformation movement take some quantum leaps of influence for the glory of the Lord Jesus Christ and fulfill our role in his greater Kingdom work as his return approaches.

J. Thomas Pelt
Ashland, Kentucky

Publishers' Preface

IT IS a privilege to publish J. Thomas Pelt's first book, *What's Right with the Church of God*. Tom is a visionary young pastor whose congregation is accomplishing great things for the kingdom of God. His ministry is an extraordinary blend of tradition and innovation.

We are distributing several books by new voices within the movement as part of celebrating the 125th anniversary of the Church of God movement in 2006–2007. They call us to think with open hearts about what the Lord would have us do in the future. Pastor Pelt is one of these new voices.

Our role with this book is somewhat different from what we usually do as a church publishing house. The author's purpose is to challenge some beliefs and practices of the Church of God, so it's inevitable that readers will disagree with him. Even our editorial staff has reservations at several points.

For example, we believe that congregational governance by a group of elders can create thorny problems for Church of God congregations (elders appointed by pastors and vice versa, self-perpetuating boards of elders, all-male boards of elders, etc.). We are not altogether comfortable with Pastor Pelt's recommendation that we abandon the camp-meeting format for state and national gatherings. And while requiring written covenants for lay leaders can help a congregation move toward a more disciplined life, it's a short step to requiring written covenants for all laity (i.e., formal church membership). We doubt that many people in the movement are ready to move in that direction.

We could tick off other points at which we disagree with the author or believe his statements should be qualified. But our purpose here is not to analyze Pastor Pelt's argument; these are simply examples of the critical discussions that we hope his book will inspire.

Pastor Pelt is a faithful servant of Christ and an emerging leader in the Church of God. He writes persuasively while being faithful to his own convictions, to the facts of church history, and to the full counsel of Holy Scripture. Therefore, we present this book to the church in spite of its disputable points—in large measure, because of them. May it stimulate personal introspection, serious contemplation of God's Word, and constructive dialogue within the Church of God movement as we reappraise our identity and our mission in the world.

The Publishers
Anderson, Indiana

1.

What Is NOT Wrong
with the Church of God

Go, stand in the temple courts, he said, and tell the people the full message of this new life. —Acts 5:20

THE MESSAGE of our movement is *not* what is wrong with the Church of God. I disagree with anyone who says that we cannot grow a fruitful and influential ministry while clearly, even proudly, proclaiming the truths of the Word of God with purposed emphasis on the doctrines of the Church of God reformation. After all, the Southern Baptists, the Assemblies of God, the Christian Church, and others are growing in influence, and they aren't a bit shy about declaring their core doctrinal beliefs. Of course, I know that there are those within the movement who not only differ to some degree on various doctrinal subjects but who believe that having an open mind in doctrinal belief and application is itself thoroughly Church of God. I somewhat disagree with the latter assertion. I believe that there is an identifiable and historically consistent thread of teaching on several key points that is woven throughout the fabric of our theological DNA (e.g., salvation, unity, holiness, spiritual gifts, end times, and divine healing); however, this book is not meant to address what has already been made clear in many worthy books. Again, my fundamental argument is that we can grow a local body without hiding our core beliefs and doctrines under a bushel. How do we do this? Purposefully, progressively, and peacefully.

If doctrinal clarity is to be communicated in a local ministry, it must be done puposefully. This is not going to happen by osmosis or merely because the sign outside the building reads Church of God. Nor will it occur merely because the preacher hits a doctrinal bull's-eye in every message. No, there must be both a unified philosophy and subsequent effort among the pastoral and lay-leadership team that not only affirm that doctrinal distinctives have a place in our broader theology but also that the broader theology stands little chance of being accurate without them. Further, I believe that this purposeful sense of doctrinal teaching will not be a source of disunity or keep seekers from seeking any further. It will be respected, if not thoroughly embraced by most people. May I also assert that no amount of methodological relevance will make up for a lack of doctrinal clarity. When seeking to be relevant as an end to itself, we end up being relevantly and relatively shallow, serving up a one-course, anemic diet of spiritual milk from the bottle (and skim milk at that) while imagining ourselves to be serving steak.

We must also share the message of the Church of God progressively. I want people to get their first dose of doctrine on their first visit to our congregation. Now mind you, they don't need a doctrinal extraction, implant, or transplant. But they should receive at least an informed consultation, accompanied by plenty of literature from the patients' lobby. Consider a general strategy:

1. *Lay Leadership.* Our success rises and falls with lay leadership. Knowing this, one of the key points of our elders' and lay leaders' covenants at Ashland is this: "Set an example in unity and harmony with the leadership, doctrines and practices of the Church of God." In establishing this as a litmus test for those leading the flock, the value of doctrinal understanding and harmony is given its rightful place of prominence. Is there agreement on every point, to every degree, and at all times? Of course not. But there needs to be a respect for the fact that this is a Church of God congregation and ministry.

2. *Assimilation.* From the literature on the tables in each breezeway to the welcome-to-the-family portion of each service, our congregation clearly communicates the message as to what kind of church we are and what we believe. More often than not, I share in the worship service, "And this much I want you to know about the Church of God. We believe that salvation in Jesus Christ alone makes you a member of God's church. If you know him as your Lord and Savior, then your

name is already written in the only roll book that will ever matter, the Lamb's Book of Life! And that roll book is good enough for us. Right, Church?" (An affirming amen is always the response!)

Prominently displayed and liberally distributed among new individuals and families at our weekly guest reception following each Sunday service are pieces of literature such as *The Church of God as Revealed in Scripture*, by Dr. Arlo Newell, and pamphlets supplied by our national offices, such as *Meet Us at the Cross* and *Who is the Church of God?* We use these in particular in our basic discipleship ministry course, Wildwood Journey, in which two, two-hour sessions are dedicated to familiarizing each disciple with the doctrinal basics of the Church of God reformation. Additionally, we make these available at our bimonthly newcomers' dinner, a catered dinner for all of our new folks. As the main course is completed and dessert is on the way, I simply pull up a stool and open the floor for questions. Inevitably, there are doctrinal questions like, What do you believe about tongues? or Do you all believe in the rapture? I do my best to keep it brief as I joyfully seize the opportunity to share the perspective of the Church of God on these topics. I often lead the conversation to this summary statement: "Having studied many doctrinal perspectives shared by numerous denominations, I believe that the doctrinal perspective we hold best positions us to fulfill the Great Commission." I have yet to have anyone walk out, and precious few have ever indicated to me that they chose not to continue worshiping with us as a result of our clearly shared and firmly held beliefs. New members are encouraged to surf our Web site as well as link to various Church of God state, national, and global sites.

3. *Preaching.* This one is easy. We need to preach our doctrine —just preach it—courageously, consistently, clearly, confidently, and with a joy that comes from a humble assurance deep within. While we are at it, we can quote liberally from Church of God sources. Speaking of which, be blessed by this quote from F. G. Smith concerning the power of pure gospel preaching:

Many hundreds of holy ministers, laboring as did the apostles of old, are at this hour preaching the pure gospel all over the earth; and it is being accepted by thousands. This preaching appeals to the spiritual-minded everywhere, because it really sets forth the whole gospel. Here we find perfect salvation and deliverance from the power of sin, with the result that pure, holy lives are led; here we find entire sanctification through the baptism of the Holy Ghost taught in the New Testament; when afflicted, we find healing for our bodies, as in the apostolic days; here we find the love, harmony, and unity of saints in one body, as exemplified in the New Testament church; here we find the entire truth. Glory to God! Here under the preaching of the pure Word by the power and inspiration of the Holy Ghost, sinners are melted to tears, and fall upon their faces, even in the public congregation, and cry to God for salvation. Here believers are baptized with the Holy Spirit and streams of holy fire descend from heaven into the congregation of saints.Ɔ

As you heed this call to preach, do so with a sincere sensitivity. In other words, build a bridge for your hearers who have never heard the Church of God perspective, then prayerfully walk with them over any divide. Again, please be prayerful and careful at this point. Most Church of God pastors have no trouble preaching the doctrinal truth, but some of us fail to do so in a spirit that builds a bridge of understanding. Rather, their spirit in preaching the truth seems to post a sign that reads, Bridge Out! Remember to match your admonishment, if not exceed it, with a heavy dose of encouragement from a heart of love for those the Spirit is seeking.

4. *Discipleship.* We need to teach it. For years I have taught a doctrinal series at least once a year using *The Church of God as Revealed in Scripture*, by Dr. Arlo Newell. I also teach several other series on specific doctrines, such as end times and sanctification, using other respected

---

1. F. G. Smith, *What the Bible Teaches* (Anderson, IN: Gospel Trumpet Co., 1914), 320.

works by Church of God authors. I do so with a spirit of anticipation; that is, I simply assume that people are hungry for truth, especially those who have had little to no biblical teaching at all or have only heard it from one denominational perspective all of their lives. Their spiritual eyes widen and then begin to glisten like those of a child as they see the Word in fresh ways.

Our doctrines should not be shared defensively—not as a reaction to some supposed sense of attack from the larger, mainline denominations and their differing interpretations. Besides, most of them are too busy planting churches and expanding their influence for the glory of the Lord even to notice us on this point, let alone engage in debate.

And don't always share doctrine with apocalyptic doom-and-gloom or do-or-die overtones of fire and brimstone. Yes, there is a place for pointing out the eternal consequence of not heeding the truth, and we do well to raise our voices and show some passion at such times, but that should not be the approach every time we share doctrine. Consider teaching doctrine to be like serving dinner at a five-star restaurant: We should lay out the finest place settings and keep it from becoming a food fight. Consider the value of superb presentation!

5. *Fellowship.* This method of teaching doctrine is more intangible, but no less real. You see, when people develop a mutual trust in a warm and lasting fellowship, they feel freer to share who they are and what they believe. So don't be afraid to be *koinonia* crazy! Provide ample opportunity to get together and just be the church in all of her love and grace. Are you planning a new facility? Be sure to plan specialized and generous spaces just for this purpose. I am convinced that the same Spirit who guides your fellowship also builds your discipleship.

We should share our doctrine peacefully. Some of this sense has already been given; however, allow me to emphasize this point with a personal illustration:

"Doctor" Tad Swift taught our largest adult discipleship group (Sunday school class) for about a year and a half. And guess what? Tad couldn't have been more dyed-in-the-wool Southern Baptist than if it was tattooed across his forehead! He firmly believed in Calvinistic doctrines such as predestination and perseverance. So what in the world was he doing teaching in a Church of God congregation? I'll tell you what he was doing. He was blessing, inspiring, informing, and altogether growing an eager group of disciples, that's what! You see, Tad and I shared far more in common than one might think. We both shared a tremendous hunger to see people saved and possessed a hunger for the Word of God. (Tad's hunger almost bordered on a perpetual sense of starvation!) In his teaching, he was as studied as he was simple and sweet, and as sweet as he was sure. Sure of what, you may ask. Predestination? Perseverance? No, although his personal theology held to these ideas, everyone knew that, first and foremost, he was sure that Jesus is the only way to eternal life. We were sure that he loved his new church family, the body of believers known as the Church of God. Although Tad was my elder in age and had been teaching the Word longer than I have been alive, he respected me as the senior pastor of the congregation. He respected my insistence on Church of God doctrine and he did not bring controversy on specific topics into his class. We simply agreed that there was a millennia's worth of Bible study to be done without constantly skating on doctrinal thin ice. He even asked me to put this understanding in writing. I did, and he agreed. We shared life together, cried together, prayed together, and got to know one another over an all-too-short couple of years. Tad was and is my dear brother. We probably weren't going to see eye to eye on this side of heaven, but that did not keep us from sharing the yoke of ministry and plowing ahead together toward an abundant harvest. You say you want things thoroughly Church of God in your congregation? I believe this partnership was the Church of God at its finest.

One more note about our Brother Tad: He has gone to be with the Lord since I began writing this book. During his last earthly days, a rare blood disorder left him with a droop in his face and forehead, so much so that it was increasingly difficult for him to keep his eyebrows from falling over his eyelids. Tad's family found him on more than one occasion sitting at his reading table, Bible and commentaries at hand, with his eyebrows taped up to his forehead just so he could continue to read and study the blessed Word of God. Oh, dear God, give me such devotion!

Of course, you can never be Church of God enough for some people—not in the doctrinal sense, anyway. For all of our emphasis, I am quite certain that we would fail the litmus test of some people in the quantity, if not the quality, of our teaching. However, for others, we are too Church of God and not seeker-sensitive enough. I have been told so numerous times. These opposite criticisms of the same ministry have been comical to me. To answer these critics, I can only offer the wisdom of comedian Bill Cosby, who says, "I do not know the secret to success, but I do know that the secret to failure is trying to please everybody."

The point of this chapter is simple: If my ministry or yours is failing to bear spiritual fruit, it may be due to many factors. However, the problem is most likely with me or you, the messengers. As applied to the whole, the message of the Church of God is definitely *not* what's wrong with our movement, but what is so blessedly right.

2.

What Problem?

So, if you think you are standing firm, be careful that you don't fall! —1 Corinthians 10:12

I recall one Halloween night several years ago that turned out to be all trick and no treat. My student ministries pastor and his family joined us for the evening. The ladies took the kids out on the quest for candy, leaving the men at our house to pass out the treats. This was mistake number one. It didn't take long for my lazy nature to get the best of me. So, instead of making repeated trips to the door, we sat down on the steps that led up to our porch, with buckets of goodies in hand.

After awhile, I heard a siren in the distance. "Do you hear that, Peter?" I asked. "Sounds like a car alarm somewhere…"

We continued our conversation concerning (what else?) our ministry. A minute or so later, a group of children hurriedly approached, bags in hands. A little princess spoke up quickly and rather nervously for the group: "Trick or treat…your house is on fire."

How cute. Still ignorant of the gravity of the moment, I calmly replied, "No, honey. We have electronic candles in the windows." This was mistake number two.

She insistently replied, pointing her finger at the picture window of the family room, "No, sir, your house is on fire!"

I turned to discover that the little girl was not trying to be cute. That car alarm in the distance was really the fire alarm in our front hallway. The fireplace mantle and the wall were already on fire. By the time we began the firefight, the flames were flashing on the ceiling. We furiously beat the flames with nearby blankets and, I believe, God graciously put the fire out. By then, fire engines were on the scene and the real firefighters rushed in to find the crisis had abated. After checking the walls and upstairs rooms, they finally gave us the all clear.

The sad part is that it took a stranger—a child, no less—to make me aware of the danger of the very real fire in my own home. (It didn't help the cause for our neighbor to later tell my ever-patient wife, "I heard your fire alarm going off and wondered why Tom just sat there!")

Some Church of God pastors still want to yawn, stretch, and say, "Problem? What problem? We've had well over a century of existence and the Church of God is still going strong! Why, our local church is doing just fine." So goes the refrain of the resting redeemed throughout our movement.

The problem is, neither the heavenly hosts nor the statistics will agree with this assessment. No, I believe that the heavenly hosts are singing quite a different tune because their perspective reveals a picture that is far from a "mighty reformation sweeping o'er the land." Want stats? Simply get out a few editions of our annual Church of God yearbook from over the years. Find your own congregation, district, and state. Then consider your numbers and those of our movement as a whole (in North America). Please, take the time to do this. You may even wish to call the Congregational Ministries office and request still more information. As you crunch the numbers, you may have a very different perspective from mine and thus come to a very different conclusion; however (and forgive my confidence at this point), I doubt it. I would further suggest that the extent of this movement's influence in North America and around the world does not reflect even remotely what our pioneers envisioned. Problem? What problem? Let's get a prophetic perspective:

> Woe to you who are complacent in Zion, and to you who feel secure on Mount Samaria, you notable men of the foremost nation, to whom the people of Israel come! Go to Calneh and look at it; go from there to great Hamath, and then go down to Gath in Philistia. Are they better off than your two kingdoms? Is their land larger than yours? You put off the evil day and bring near a reign of terror. You lie on beds

inlaid with ivory and lounge on your couches. You dine on choice lambs and fattened calves. You strum away on your harps like David and improvise on musical instruments. You drink wine by the bowlful and use the finest lotions, but you do not grieve over the ruin of Joseph. Therefore you will be among the first to go into exile; your feasting and lounging will end. (Amos 6:1–7)

We may resent these remarks, but only because we well represent them. While we are at it, we might as well let another prophet rub salt in our wounds:

From the least to the greatest, all are greedy for gain; prophets and priests alike, all practice deceit. They dress the wound of my people as through it were not serious…Obey me, and I will be your God and you will be my people. Walk in all the ways I command you, that it may go well with you. But they did not listen or pay attention; instead, they followed the stubborn inclinations of their evil hearts. They went backward and not forward. (Jer 6:13–14; 7:23–24)

Are we deceived about the desperate state of our movement? Are we even semiconsciously deceiving ourselves from within? Actually, I rather hope so. God forbid that we would consciously know our state and simply not care enough to take concerted and united action! Further (and this should be no solace), our friends in various denominations are in the same sad state.

Are we listening? Are we paying attention? Church of God, our wound is serious. Our house is on fire. An alarm is going off, and it is not the distant sound of someone else's crisis.

Dearly beloved, the Spirit of God is raising his voice! The statistical realities are begging our urgent attention. We must not refuse to face the facts. What facts are those? For the purpose of this discussion, I would boil them down to three:

First, the Church of God is indeed ordained of God as a vital part of his greater Kingdom work in these last days. (In retrospect and with the benefit of more than a century of greater light, we are not likely the *only* true work of God, as claimed by some Church of God preachers in our earlier days. This claim ought to stir some folks up. If so, my work here is done).

Second, we have not nearly fulfilled the extent of the vision cast by our movement's pioneers. In other words, yes, we do have a problem!

Third, *we must act now.* "Do not say, 'Four months more and then the harvest?' I tell you, open your eyes and look at the fields! They are ripe for harvest" (John 4:35).

3.

The Blame Game

For whoever keeps the whole law and yet stumbles at just one point is guilty of breaking all of it. —James 2:10

L ET'S GET this out of the way. Let's really point some fingers and be done with it! Just whose fault is the decline of the Church of God in North America anyway?

Obviously, it is the general director's fault. No, wait...that position hasn't been in existence long enough to blame. Besides, the General Assembly put him in that position.

That's it! The General Assembly is to blame for our lack of recent progress. No, wait...the GA is made up mostly of our frontline pastors and lay leaders who are giving it all they've got. Besides, they only meet once a year.

Maybe it's really a systemic or structural problem. That's it...our structure is to blame. Let's call a big meeting, then, and restructure! No, please, not another symposium, think tank, focus group, or open forum to vote on a less than resolute mandate.

Yet we feel someone has to take the blame. Someone ought to be sitting in the hot seat.

Maybe it's a combination of culprits. Perhaps it's due to the sometimes cleverly cloaked conflicts between our many entities, such as the Ministries Council, the Pastors Fellowship, the National Association, the Concilio, our colleges, or the Andersonian leaders of our movement. Are their turf wars really to blame? No, many efforts toward reconciliation are bringing about slow, but sure, change in and among the diverse divides of these groups. Our leaders should be commended for the efforts made in the past decade toward greater unity.

"Still, somebody is to blame," you may say, "and it's not me!"

We insist that unity is one of the flames symbolizing our movement. Dare we admit that each of us see too many *thems*, such that a truly unified *we* is little more than part of our logo? Come now, such a continued denial of responsibility does not become a people intellectually, let alone spiritually. Excuse me for a moment while I sing a familiar tune:

> You will notice we say "brother and sister" 'round here—
> It's because we're a family and these folks are so near.
>
> When one has a heartache we all share the tears,
> And rejoice in each victory in this family so dear.[1]

Oh, yeah, that's who we are! The family of God! Indeed we are. But we should know ourselves and our emotional tendencies better than to fall for our own siren song. A couple of verses of this (and I mean no offense, Brother and Sister Gaither... I have always been a big fan!), and we will just break into another singspiration, testify awhile, hug a few necks, wipe a few tears, and then scatter to the four winds until next year's camp meeting or convention.

No! We must deal with the issue, lest our very real divisions be our demise. If we are who we preach, teach, write, and sing that we are, then we cannot merely coexist as *us* and *them*. And if we continue thinking and living this way, we need look no further for someone to blame. *We* are to blame. And that *we* includes you and me.

"God, forgive me for all of the times my *me* and *mine* have gotten in the way of the *you* and *yours* that the world is just waiting for me to share. And thank you for making me a part of your family, in spite of myself!"

Strides have indeed been made in the direction of genuine Christian unity. Let us continue down this path.

I recall counseling two couples with shared children and stepchildren. Things were really getting ugly (secret videotapes, public confrontations, court battles, etc.). Of course, the kids were the ones really beginning to suffer. Having counseled them in any and every way I knew how—admonishing, nurturing, instructing, and trying to preserve the

---

1. "The Family of God," words by William J. Gaither and Gloria Gaither.

peace for more than a year—I finally stopped them in the middle of what would be our last session and just yelled (and I mean really *yelled*), "Stop it, just stop it! You are killing your kids and wearing me out! Everyone who knows you is sick of it and sick of you. This is pathetic!"

I told them that I and other pastors, counselors, family members, and friends had given them all of the love, prayers, and advice they could ever want or need, but at some point, they would have to decide that enough is enough and just determine to get along with one another. And they had better do it before irreparable collateral damage was done to the children.

Suddenly, they had an epiphany. A light bulb went on over these two couples' heads. They realized that this war between them had, sadly, become their very identity. It was their chosen reality, their constant excuse for all of their ills, their all-consuming motivation for their low-level living. Did some of their disagreements remain? Yes. However, they began to put their pettiness behind them and the Lord and the kids first. They have enjoyed a greater season of harmony since. End of counseling.

Family of God, is this us? Have we begun to define ourselves by our divisions? Worse, have we used this identity as an excuse for our own ills and low-level living?

Certainly, some very real disagreements led to decisions that perpetuated our divisions. No one denies that. And some of those divisive decisions were made in the genuine interest of and hope for some semblance of peace. But is peace merely the absence of conflict? Come on, aren't we being just a little pathetic ourselves? We should be embarrassed and just plain tired of it, tired of ourselves.

Let's stop the blame game—just stop it! We are breaking the heart of the Father and damaging, not merely this generation, but our spiritual children and grandchildren. Woe unto us as we do so! (See Luke 17:1–2.)

Before continuing, read James 4:1–10. May we all take this passage personally and heed its counsel.

4.

Prayerlessness

After they prayed, the place where they were meeting was shaken. And they were all filled with the Holy Spirit and spoke the Word of God boldly. —*Acts 4:31*

TELL ME, when is the last time you attended a prayer meeting? "Why, Brother Pelt, we have prayer meeting every week!" Do you? Please forgive me, but I think not, not by New Testament or Church of God heritage standards. Just what, then, is a real prayer meeting?

First, let me tell you with certainty what it is not. Prayer meeting is not the habitual and sometimes zombie-like gathering of God's people on Sunday or Wednesday evening that is opened with a quick prayer, followed by a much lengthier time of announcements, followed by singing (first, second, and last verses only, please), maybe some testimony and prayer requests, followed by another pastoral pontification in prayer, a musical special, then a lesson by the pastor, and closes with another brief word of prayer. I'm not sure this is necessarily God's idea of corporate worship in general, but I am confident it has never described a true prayer meeting.

Prayer meeting is the purposeful gathering of God's people marked by persevering, persistent, perspiring, painful, powerful, praying through kinds of prayer. It is determined and it is desperate. It is bold and it is burdensome. It is "joy unspeakable and full of glory!" It is quiet, still, and somber. It is loud, dynamic, and energized. It is not time-conscious, space-conscious, seeker-friendly, or other-conscious. Rather, prayer meeting is conscious only of our lack and God's sufficiency, of our sin (mostly of omission!) and his righteousness. As Oswald Chambers said, "Prayer does not prepare us for the greater works, prayer is the greater work."[1] And this reveals one of the most fundamental reasons why even greater work has yet to be done in and through the Church of God movement. We Church of God folks meet, greet, eat, preach, teach, sing, eat again, vision, plan, strategize, discuss, debate, table the discussion, then have dessert, schedule the next meeting, and leave...but we do not pray! So what's the solution? The solution is a vital prayer ministry in every congregation, saturating every work done in the name of our Lord Jesus Christ.

Prayer ministry is fundamental to all other ministries. It should be targeted and widespread throughout all other endeavors. It will look a little different in every congregation but have much in common with others. It will grow, evolve, and change. God will show his favor and blessing in direct proportion to your earnestness in prayer ministry. (Actually, he will bless far beyond your prayerful efforts!) Before sharing with you some practical prayer ministry ideas, let me share with you a testimony to its power.

Prayer ministry was one of our first priorities as we partnered together with First Church of God in Ashland, Kentucky, several years ago. I determined that each Wednesday night, we would not share announcements, take prayer requests, give testimonies, sing, teach, or preach. No, we would come together and pray, seeking God's will for our ministry in a humility that reflected our cluelessness as to God's exact direction for us. In addition, our lay-leadership meetings (at that time, consisting of the trustees and church council) would be marked by the same purposeful seasons of prayer for the will of God. This emphasis pervaded the rest of our ministry and continues today, and it can most certainly be credited as the basis for all of the growth and momentum we have attained.

The time came to get serious about making room for more, as we called it, even though we still had some room left, according to the fire marshal. So we did. Over the next couple of months, we began to sort through all of our options, beginning with an expansion of present facili-

---

1. Oswald Chambers, *My Utmost for His Highest,* October 17.

ties. In fact, this was our most favored option. To this end, we continued in fervent prayer. On one occasion, I split our leadership team into groups. One group stayed inside, and the other went outside and fanned out around the property. I instructed our lay leaders to go ahead and believe God for expanded territory—just go ahead and claim it, speak it! I told them that all God could say is no, which only means yes to something better. Of particular interest to me was a park adjacent to us, just beyond our lower parking lot. Wildwood Park had always been owned by the A. K. Steele Corporation. I was in the group who claimed this acreage for the Kingdom. I remember asking my group, as we finished praying and walked inside, "Do you think they would sell it?" Although full of faith, several in the group admitted that was very unlikely. In further discussion with the rest of the group, most agreed. However, I felt I had to push this issue: "How do we know? Has anyone asked?" So, we did.

Over the next couple of months, we made two inquiries, by letter and in person, to the corporate headquarters. Both times, the response was the same. They had no inclination to sell the property, in whole or in part, now or in the future. We had been persistent, but the owners were most clear and we took this as another closed door that would bring us even closer to the real answer. We turned our attention to our present facility. Maybe we could remodel and expand the sanctuary. Our lay leaders recalled considering this option before and, after some specific investigation of our structure, we came to the same conclusion they had before. This option was not feasible due to the many code restrictions concerning the building itself, parking, and other infrastructure requirements.

Again, no problem. We would simply do what the congregation had done on several occasions in its history in order to facilitate growth: We would look for land, move, and build! This was an exciting time. We considered about five area properties of ten to twenty acres each. However, only one of these properties really seemed right; it was a former Lowe's home improvement store on sixteen acres of land.

The more we looked it over, the better it looked. An on-site tour with company officials and the present tenants confirmed our conclusion that this had the potential to be more than we had even imagined. And the location couldn't have been better! It was on Route 60, the busiest thoroughfare in our area! Our excitement continued to build as we went into the contract phase, and the price of $1.6 million didn't scare the leadership, either. We believed God would provide. A closing date was set and all seemed to be going well.

Then the occupying tenants of the facility changed their tune. They weren't eager to honor their contract with Lowe's, which required them to vacate the property after appropriate notice. They tried to exercise their right of first refusal (seek a purchase contract before others were considered), but their funding did not work out. Nevertheless, they were determined to hang onto the property, even if it meant legal action. Meanwhile, they launched a public relations campaign against us. Flyers were distributed, letters to the newspaper editor were written, and the gossip mill ran at full tilt. People imagined the big, mean church was kicking the tenants out and putting their employees out of work. They talked about shattered dreams, starving children in the streets—you get the picture. Thankfully, most people in the community took all of this with a grain of salt and continued to encourage us to stay the course. We continued to honor the purchase contract we had signed and looked forward to the closing date.

However, in the business world, money talks. Unknown to us, another group was enticing the owners with serious money—cash money. Of course, having a contract, this really meant little. So we naïvely thought. We assumed that the owners would honor our contract. However, they began to show signs that they would rather deal with the new buyers. Our contacts were increasingly out of town and generally unavailable. Our phone calls, e-mails, and letters went unanswered. We began to pray fervently about the whole deal. Yes, we were willing to do whatever it took to expand the kingdom of God. We knew we had conducted ourselves above reproach, but nothing was worth soiling the reputation of the Master in the eyes of the public. Still full of faith, but truly disappointed, we pulled the plug on the transaction through a series of Monday night calls to our trustees. Admittedly, we had a strange sense of relief, but also the sense that the wind had died, leaving the sails of our gospel ship limp and lifeless. But a God thing was about to happen in answer to prayer.

Two days later, I was driving up to the church building when my eyes were drawn by something new on the fence next to our property. There was a sign that read: For Sale, Wildwood Park, 85+ Acres. Surely, I was seeing things! I stopped, put the old Jeep in a quick reverse and backed up to the sign just to make sure my eyes hadn't deceived me. Sure enough, the park that we had claimed in prayer, the same property that was denied us twice, was now for sale!

I called our trustee board chairperson and church council vice-chair that very day. Of course, calls from members of our congregation began coming in, and many approached me that night at church service, saying, "Did you see the sign? Well, are you going to check it out?" Of course! We jumped all over that deal and had a purchase contract on it within a couple of weeks. And the price was right—$700,000 for the land, buildings, shelters, tractors, equipment, and all!

"Unbelievable!"

"Wow!"

"You have got to be kidding!"

"Praise the Lord!"

"Hallelujah!"

We could not say enough to describe our emotions and our gratitude for this remarkable move of God. Even more, the whole community was behind us. Civic leaders from council members to the mayor, school officials, and charitable organizations contacted me to express their pleasure at the prospect of our owning the park. Of course, all of them hoped that we would be open to partnering with them in the park's use, and we assured them of our sincere desire to do just that. Since then, we have acquired the park and prayed and prayed and prayed over it. We have walked in and throughout its length and breadth, anointing with oil as we go. We have connected with so many people throughout the tri-state area through its use. We can scarcely contain our enthusiasm as we begin to envision the possibilities for ministry in the future! Prayer works! It really, really works!

Please, would you allow this testimony to motivate you to launch your own prayer ministry? There are, certainly, better models. I urge you to contact our National Prayer Ministry (see www.chog.org) to find out about others, but perhaps you can take our local ministry as one example.

We begin with team leaders. Each one is responsible for the formation of a prayer ministry team. This team is made up of those who have an informed passion for prayer ministry. By informed, I simply mean that they know what they are getting themselves into—not the mere administrative updating of a prayer-chain list. Rather, the prayer ministry team engages in the challenging and sometimes exhaustive work of equipping and engaging, by example, our entire ministry in prayer works of all types. We invest in these team leaders with training resources, planning meetings, and, of course, seasons of prayer!

Knowing that prayer works, we encourage our people to undertake all different types of prayer. No doubt, most of these are already familiar to you in theory, but the practice of some types of prayer may still await some assertive action in your congregation.

Personal Prayer. We don't come together for prayer empty-handed. Each member of the body of Christ must realize the need for and persistently relish the daily discipline of prayer. This is especially true for lay leaders and pastoral staff. E. E. Byrum said,

> The pathway of the divine life is paved with prayer. No one can make spiritual progress without it. Where you find a true saint of God who is a power in his hands you will find one who knows enough about the real worth of prayer to be found often pleading with God, sending up earnest petitions and receiving answers, and pouring out his heart in gratitude and thankfulness to him for his abundant mercies. What riches there are to be obtained, and what blessings are bestowed in answer to an humble, fervent prayer![2]

---

2. E. E. Byrum, *The Secret of Salvation* (Moundsville, WV: Gospel Trumpet Co., 1896), 156–157.

Pastor's Prayer Warriors. Each pastoral staff member would be greatly blessed by gathering a select group of Aarons and Hurs (see Exodus 17:12) to prayerfully support them and hold them accountable. I have a group of about twelve prayer warriors that I call my Pastor's PAC. This stands for *power, accountability,* and *courage.* They pray that I will have power to carry out my calling; accountability for my thoughts, words, and deeds; and victory over the temptations of money, sex, and power; and courage to boldly lead the congregation's ministry according to the vision God has given us. These pastor's prayer warriors diligently pray for me and with me at the front of the sanctuary before each worship service. They pray that my preaching and teaching will be void of self and full of the Holy Spirit. And they pray in increasing measure as I preach and approach a time of decision. They pray over my daily schedule of appointments, using my vision and planning worksheet that I share with them in confidence.

One more task has to do with the blameless standard we are to hold as spiritual elders: I have one of my prayer warriors act as my shadow while I am at church for worship services or special events. By doing so, this person is an encouragement to me by providing personal fellowship and serves as an extra set of eyes and ears, ready to run interference and serve as a witness to any personal interaction I may have.

Worship Prayer Warriors. Quoting British poet Martin Tupper, Charles Spurgeon wrote, "Prayer is the slender nerve that moveth the muscles of omnipotence."[3] When we consider some of the great ministries and ministers of the gospel—beginning with the Apostles of the first-century church, through the great reformers and revivalists, right up to the evangelists of today—do we believe there is a secret to unleashing powerful moves of the Spirit, especially in our times of corporate worship? No, it is no secret! We understand what happened, when we carefully read Luke's account in Acts and do even a casual study of celebrated communicators of the gospel, such as John Wesley, Charles Spurgeon, Charles Finney, D. L. Moody, and Billy Graham, as well

---

3. Cited in Charles Spurgeon, *Salt-Cellars*, vol. 1, 1889, 114.

as our movement's own greats, such as D. S. Warner, A. L. Byers, and Lillie McCutcheon. Our study would certainly reveal that the common thread, tediously and tightly woven throughout their lives and ministries, was prayer. History records a direct correlation between mighty moves of God as these servants spoke the Word and the simultaneous and sacrificial prayers of select prayer partners.

In our ministry at Ashland, the Spirit is moving in ways that are unprecedented. I am seeing conviction, confession, salvation, healing, restoration, deliverance, encouragement, and freedom as I have never experienced. Everyone wants to know why. What are we doing that is so different? Let me assure you that it is not because my powers of persuasion are so effective. (That thought is comic to me!) And it is not because we are blessed with incredibly gifted worship leaders, musicians, and singers (even though we are). It is not because we have plenty of money, because we operate, largely, week to week in faith. No, if we are doing anything that is qualitatively and quantitatively different, it is praying!

Let me challenge you—sort of pick a fight with you spiritually—by saying that perhaps you just aren't needy enough, not humble enough. You don't realize (or you refuse to admit) just how needy you truly are. Could it be that you aren't spiritually hungry enough—as a pastor, as a congregation, and especially your lay leaders? (This is huge!)

Perhaps you aren't upset enough, either—not upset enough to say, "No, things are not okay! And we aren't putting up with it anymore! People must be drawn to Christ! People must be saved, healed, restored, renewed, discipled, disciplined, challenged, changed, excited, and encouraged! And we will doggedly insist on it, starting with prayer!"

Desperation among God's people accompanies all great movements of God. May I suggest that you aren't desperate enough yet?

You see, once you have tasted such an extraordinary move of the Holy Spirit, you are spoiled for anything less. Please, try enlisting prayer warriors first, instead of another change in curriculum, style, or leadership. You won't have any less work to do, but you may be more pleased with the results. Enough said.

If you are willing to try launching a ministry of worship prayer warriors, let me propose how you might go about it: As the worship center begins to fill, our worship prayer warriors begin to go to war (that is, pray). Some prayer warriors are in their seats and they are praying Scripture. They simply turn to a powerful promise in Scripture and claim it now, for this moment in time. Some of them are reading the Psalms aloud, vocally filling the worship center with ancient echoes of praise and thanksgiving. Some are prayer walking—discreetly walking around the worship center while praying heaven down! Others are kneeling at the altars praying individually. Still more have called impromptu circles of prayer, meeting at the front of the sanctuary or in their section of the worship center. There they pray, one at a time or in a united chorus. Another group is meeting in the prayer room. They may not join us in the worship center that day; they will not cease giving praise and thanksgiving, making intercession, or opposing the influence of the Enemy until that morning's battle is over. This is our continually changing and ever evolving worship prayer warriors' ministry, and it works!

Power Pauses. Often throughout the week, our office staff, pastors, volunteers, and maybe even our cleaning service—whoever happens to be in close proximity—are called together for an impromptu season of prayer. We call this a power pause. We may stop, drop what we're doing, and praise the Lord or lift up a specific need. We may put one of the ministry team in the mercy seat (see below). Whatever the case, we are instant and constant in prayer, and lots of it!

Of course, some critics will say, "Isn't this an interruption? Doesn't it constantly stop the church's work? Don't you have more pressing things to attend to?"

No, not really. How can taking God at his Word be an interruption? And, no, we don't have better things to do. Not if we want to be better and minister better. We get right back to doing those things after just a few minutes.

Mercy Seat. This is a blessed method of prayer based on Exodus 25:17–22 (cf. Lev 17:11). No doubt, the mercy seat is familiar to you. God's symbolic throne and seat of power, the ark of the covenant, was capped with a cover of atonement, symbolizing his great mercy. God's mercy is extended to us still today! We can use a chair to remind us of his presence. Simply use a chair during your season of prayer to take turns sitting in the mercy seat. As each person is seated, cover that person with the laying on of hands and anointing of oil. Pray fervently for the person on the mercy seat. Then thank God for his great mercy!

Twenty-Four Hours of Power. Once a quarter, we have a twenty-four-hour prayer meeting in the worship center. In preparation, we provide prayer cards in the Sunday bulletin and on the tables in each breezeway. We choose a theme (e.g., prayers for salvation, prayers for our nation to be called back to God, prayers for physical healing), or we just leave the agenda wide open. People write their requests on these cards and bring them to the platform, where they are laid across the width of the stage. The Twenty-Four Hours of Power begins at noon on Friday and goes until noon on Saturday. Music for praise and worship plays in the background as God's people come to pray. Many come to the front of the sanctuary and pray over each card. Others may take a card and walk throughout the sanctuary. Still others take several request cards and find a place to sit and pray. Several gather for a circle of prayer. Regardless of the manner, the people of God come together and they pray, pray, pray. The pastoral staff and the elders sign up on a sheet, taking two-hour shifts to oversee this prayer time and set the pace as leaders. This prayer meeting gets God's attention as much as any event I have seen. Sometimes I wonder why we don't do this once a month.

Prayer Meeting. Remember how we described a prayer meeting earlier? Well, why not start one? Just show up one Sunday evening or Wednesday night, in Sunday school or at small group and go for it! Remember, you don't make announcements, you don't sing, you don't preach or teach, and you don't take prayer requests or gather an offering. You simply meet as the people of God and pray as we were born to. We have had groups meeting for prayer even on Friday nights, beginning at 10:00! They sometimes pray for hours for one of our ministries. Is there any wonder why there is such an anointing of God's Spirit?

What about your main worship service on Saturday night or Sunday morning? Would such a prayer meeting be a hindrance to the plan? Absurd. Try this: Do your normal bulletin-ordained stuff to get it out of God's way. Then, instead of preaching, lead your people in a season of prayer—lead them in corporate prayer, lead in a prayer walk, lead a concert of prayer. Some people may pray at the altars, some may stand at the front of the sanctuary, some may walk in prayer around the sanctuary. Let go! (Since when did you have to be in complete control, anyway?) Come on, trust the Lord and trust his Word. The people of God will get it. Their spirits will remember that this used to be normal. Their spiritual muscle memory will come back as they begin the exercise. Relax; the saints will embrace a prayer meeting. What about the seekers? It's perfect! They will have a chance, maybe for the first time, to truly see the church in its natural environment—that of prayer.

Praying Leaders. Our elders are praying people. Not only are they so in the personal sense but also in the united sense as leaders. Our elders each have a day of the week when they fast and pray for our ministry. The greater church family is aware of this fact, and many have joined them in this lifestyle. With this united effort in prayer, it is no wonder to me that our times of conducting the Father's business as ministry leaders are so full of his Spirit.

Prayer Retreat. Get away to a conference center, a Church of God campground, or a local park and pray. If you like, ask a special guest to give your people some training in prayer. Just don't forget to pray!

We need to consider one essential ingredient for prevailing prayer, and that is purity of life, holiness. Any unconfessed or unrepented sin will block the connection with God. Jim Cymbala speaks well to this point in his recent book *Breakthrough Prayer*. He writes,

> A clear conscience and a pure heart are absolute necessities for prevailing prayer. I cannot confidently ask God for answers when I cling to the sins that nailed his Son to the cross of Calvary. I cannot live in iniquity and enjoy the Lord's favor simultaneously. These are impossibilities in God's moral universe. This truth highlights the enormous fallacy of teach-

ing that certain prayers bring success and blessing apart from the spiritual condition of the petitioner. Prayers taken from Scripture, even the Lord's Prayer, will be null and void if people harbor hidden sin in their hearts. "If I regard wickedness in my heart, the Lord will not hear" (Psalm 66:18 NASB).[4]

So before we seek to tackle any infirmity or spiritual stronghold through prayer, perhaps we would want to share this truth with our people and ensure that there is nothing to compromise the movement of the Spirit.

As the people of God, our natural environment is prayer. Jesus affirmed that this is the defining characteristic of our gatherings in his name and in his places of worship (see Mark 11:15–18). When we truly begin to be a praying church, we will begin to get back to normal—New Testament normal. When we fail to be so, we rob ourselves, rob the lost, and rob God of all that comes as a direct result of making prayer a viable, visible, and vocal priority throughout our ministries. "As for me, far be it from me that I should sin against the Lord by failing to pray for you" (1 Sam 12:23). Don't delay. Don't wait until you have called a meeting, conducted an interest survey, and promoted the event. Just be the church and start praying!

---

4. Jim Cymbala, *Breakthrough Prayer* (Grand Rapids, MI: Zondervan, 2003), 84.

5.

The Right Question

But when the chief priests and the teachers of the law saw the wonderful things he did and the children shouting in the temple area, "Hosanna to the Son of David," they were indignant. "Do you hear what these children are saying?" they asked him. "Yes," replied Jesus, "Have you never read, 'From the lips of children and infants you have ordained praise?'" —Matthew 21:15–16

YOU CANNOT get a right answer by asking a wrong question. So, maybe we aren't asking the right questions when it comes to dealing with our lack of influence as a movement.

Let's consider some of the wrong questions we have been asking. Perhaps "wrong" is a bit strong. However, we ask less important questions far too often and avoid more important ones, especially in leadership circles: How many are you running now? Did you go to this or that conference? Did you get a raise? Did you make budget? These are important questions, but more revealing questions concerning the health of a ministry can be asked. How many have been saved and baptized lately? How many are in your small group ministry? How's your Faith Promise giving? These are better questions to ask and continue asking.

However, there may be a more strategic question still—one that, if answered correctly, will result in the right answers to every one of the previous questions. Let me set the stage for this one. We were gathered for our first annual First Church of God Vision Conference. The leadership was prayed up, prepared to stay up, and had been studying up on their prep packet for a couple of weeks. After supper and a long season of prayer, we began our time of visioning in earnest. I opened the time by making the following statement: "Folks, we are going to vision so many wonderful and exciting things, and all will be important and strategic to the overall vision statement ('Jesus Christ: To Know Him, To Love Him, To Serve Him, To Share Him!'). However, there is one question that we must ask, and it must serve as a guiding question for our ministry until Jesus comes again. If we answer this question correctly, consistently, and quickly, we will grow. We will grow because the favor and blessing of God will be upon us. The question is this: What's here for our kids?"

This is the unspoken question of every grandparent rearing a second generation. It's the question of that single mom or dad, that young couple, and all those seeking a church home with the spiritual health and wellbeing of their kids in the forefront of their minds! The reality is this for most people as they seek a church home: You can have the best facilities, music, preaching, teaching, and more, but if your youth and children's ministries are relegated to a few special events and glorified babysitting on Sundays and Wednesdays, they will go elsewhere. If they don't, it is only due to the fact that they have been lulled to sleep with the rest of religious North America, who think having a youth group or a children's group is the same as having a youth or children's ministry. Quite simply, our mistake is in making adult ministries the focus of our local ministries. The secular world figured this one out long ago. Secular marketers know that the key to parents' hearts (or, more importantly, to their bank accounts) is through their kids. So they have learned how to capture kids' imaginations, mold their dreams, and train them subliminally to be hungry for more and more of whatever it is that the merchants have to offer. They are succeeding to the tune of billions and billions of dollars every year. Advertisers have successfully wagered that any investment made in capturing children and youth and creating their culture will bring an overwhelming return, time and time and time again. We Christians should take a cue from the marketing gurus of the secular world and make the younger generations far more of a target of our ministry efforts.

Naturally, the follow-up question is, How do we do this? How do we answer the right question?

First, we must have a change of heart. We can start by praying to be filled with the Spirit of Christ as it pertains to our ministry focus. Jesus said, "Let the children come to me" (Matt 19:14). Our children's ministry pastor shared with me a powerful book by George Barna, which, in turn, was passed on to all of our leadership. In it, Barna concludes,

> There is nothing I covet more than to someday hear the Lord say, "Well done, good and faithful servant." My assumption—never seriously challenged either by my own reflections or by the arguments of others—has been that the most efficient path toward receiving such an accolade from God would be through intense focus upon the moral development and spiritual transformation of adults.
>
> I had never given alternative approaches serious consideration. After all, aren't *adults* the ones who call the shots in the world and determine the nature of our current and future reality? If the family is central to a healthy society and a strong Church, shouldn't we invest our resources predominantly in the *adults* who lead those units? When it comes to grasping the substance, the subtleties, and the implications of the Christian faith, don't *adults* possess the greatest learning and intellectual capacities? Strategically, isn't it more important for us to equip *adults* so that they can use their gifts and resources to advance the Kingdom?
>
> No, no, no and no. In retrospect, my view was so far off the mark that I didn't just miss the boat—I missed the entire ocean![1]

We must join Barna and be transformed in heart as well as "by the renewing of our minds" (Rom 12:1–2) when it comes to the place of priority we give to youth and children's ministries.

---

1. George Barna, *Transforming Children into Spiritual Champions* (Ventura, CA: Regal Books, 2003), 11–12.

Second, we should adopt an investment mentality. Pastors and lay leaders can do this, for starters, by forbidding foul language among the people, especially the leadership. Words like *cost*, *expense*, and *expensive* should be removed from your vocabulary and replaced with the words *invest*, *investing*, and *investment*! You see, our kids aren't a cost or an expense. (Again, secular marketers don't see them this way. Why do we?) Our kids are an investment in eternity, and the returns are more than we could imagine. This is all part of the ministry strategy given by God through Moses concerning his blessed Word:

> Love the Lord your God with all your heart and with all your soul and with all your strength. These commandments that I give you today are to be upon your hearts. Impress them on your children. Talk about them when you sit at home and when you walk along the road, when you lie down and when you get up. (Deut 6:5–7)

In other words, make kids your priority. If you still don't agree with this philosophy in deference to giving adults priority, then just wait a few years. These kids will grow up and then you can have them in all of their adult glory. The question is what kind of adults will they be if you haven't invested in capturing their souls, minds, and strength for Jesus Christ while they were most tender and pliable?

Let me illustrate what I mean. When we entered into this ministry partnership in January of 2002, our congregation had no other ministry staff, yet we had ample, but very dated, space. We had a decision to make. Invest in bringing the present facilities up to date through a big renovation effort or invest in leadership, ministry, and facilities more in keeping with our guiding ministry question, What's here for our kids? After a year of praying, visioning, planning, training, equipping, and more praying, we stepped out on faith and hired two additional full-time pastors. We brought in a pastor of worship arts and administration (interesting combo, but it worked for us) and a pastor of student ministries. Our worship arts pastor immediately began spreading a first-fruits philosophy (more about this in chapter 15). We all bought into it, especially concerning student ministries (youth). We determined that we would allow our student ministries team to design the best youth ministry space anywhere in the tri-state area. About four months later, we opened the Upstream Student Ministries Youth House. It included a worship center (staging and large gathering area; video projection system; and video monitors throughout the facility for worship and discipleship); the Feeding Frenzy kitchen and café; a game room with Xbox, PlayStation 2, and pool and foosball tables; ample restrooms; a check-in/information station; a prayer room; and more.

With absolutely no apologies to critics who said this was only entertainment, we began to see big numbers of kids attending, having a blast—and confessing Christ as their Lord and Savior! Now the youth ministry averages 100 in their worship services and over 70 in small-group ministry throughout the week. To God be the glory. Our youth are worth it! My teenager is one of them. As a parent, I say, where else would I want them to be any day or night of the week? We have continued to invest by adding a media/tech center for tutoring and study after school and on weekends.

We have chosen to invest in much the same way for children's ministry. We hired a full-time children's pastor and transformed our Family Life Center into a fully functioning Children's Ministry Center. We now have more than one hundred children participating in the Kids for Christ ministry, learning to worship and grow in the Word of God. Most of the rest of our facilities are lost in the décor of the '70s (we are still covered in wood paneling), but no one seems to care. It is worth the sacrifice, worth the investment. We have experienced the favor, blessing, and fruit of the Holy Spirit since we started putting kids first.

You may be thinking, Yeah, but you are a big church with a lot more money than we have. This couldn't be further from the truth! First of all, I think a big church starts with an attendance somewhere around one thousand, and we aren't there just yet. We adopted our philosophy and prayerfully stepped out in it while we had about two hundred people in attendance. And money? After an initial investment from our savings of about $50,000 during the second year, we have done most of these things by faith. Our certificates of deposit have long since been cashed in as we invested in ministry and leadership. We now have little savings; we are just living and ministering by faith, week to week. Isn't that great? What could we possibly be saving money for, anyway? A rainy day? This is the day of the latter reign of Christ, in and through his people, so we dare not hide his money in the ground. Yes, strategically saving for future ministry initiatives is a good practice, if you genuinely intend on implementing them. This is the Joseph principle (Gen 41). However, most ministries are only hoarding to have and are not implementing Joseph's "store to pour" methodology.

> Then the man who had received the one talent came. "Master," he said, "I knew that you are a hard man, harvesting where you have not sown and gathering where you have not scattered seed. So I was afraid and went out and hid your talent in the ground. See, here is what belongs to you." (Matt 25:24–25)

Surely we recall how the Master responded to this self-serving sort of fear. No, we must invest the Master's money and roll over the eternal returns, again and again, until he comes back. You may wonder, Are your leaders fiscally responsible? Are they good stewards? Yes, to a level I have never before witnessed. They are full of faith, even when we are short of funds! Have we made some mistakes along the way? Of course, and we will make still more.

I am not advocating that a congregation burden itself with financial debt, but I would challenge you on this point: Do something. In fact, do a series of somethings. If you do ten somethings in ministry, you may mess up two or three, but that means you will have done six or seven things right! I love what Pastor Randy Montgomery told his former congregation in Lake Wales, Florida, when they asked what he would do as their leader. He replied, "I'm not sure just yet. But I do know two things I will do. I will make mistakes and it will cost you money!"

We have accomplished those two things several times over in our ministry. Yet lives have been touched, ministry influence has grown, and you can be sure that the Holy Spirit and the "bond of perfectness" (Col 3:14 KJV) among the people has sufficed to cover our messes. And the God thing continues. So I urge you to pray up, pray through, and then do something.

I am often asked, "Do big and influential ministries do what they do because they are big? Or are they big and influential because they do what they do?" I believe it is the latter. I have seen God honor the faith of ministries where people began to act like the mighty church of God, even when their resources were limited. God has blessed them with big influence, big provision, and big numbers of people!

Family of God, we must quit making excuses, especially the cleverly cloaked and cowardly excuses concerning money. We must sacrificially invest in eternity through our youth and children as never before.

6.

Traditionalism

*I was advancing in Judaism beyond many Jews of my own age
and was extremely zealous for the traditions of my fathers.*
—*Galatians 1:14*

SOMEONE has said, "What is traditional may not be biblical, and
what is biblical may not be traditional." Pause for a few minutes
and let that sink in. Perhaps you should write down a few reactions, a
couple of challenges or critiques to this assertion, and then prayerfully
discern what it may mean in your life.

This chapter will be hard medicine for many to swallow because
we have scarcely challenged the traditions of our local congregations.
We have traditional orders of worship, worship styles, special events,
unwritten and unspoken ministry philosophies, expectations, and rules
for the games that we play (whether we admit their existence or not!).
This is especially true among the leadership of most of our churches.
Why is traditionalism such a difficult and downright divisive subject?
Because it forces us to pass judgment on our past, the good ol' days.
More importantly (and more painfully), it forces us to think objectively
about those beloved people from our past whose memories are inextricably woven into the fabric of our heritage. Even the thought of doing this is, well, unthinkable! The apostle Paul acknowledged that his
zealousness in persecuting the church was directly linked to his holding
onto the traditions of his spiritual fathers (Gal 1:13–17). Perhaps because this is the case for many of us, we have just left well enough alone
in our ministries to avoid contradicting some principle of tradition or
cross some invisible line drawn by those who have gone on before us.
The problem is that well enough is just not good enough anymore. It
really never was.

Allow me to be the bad guy for a moment and make two assertions concerning the problem of traditionalism.

First, it is foolish to think that the good ol' days were as good as we remember them. Our memories are very selective. The truth is, the older we get, the better we were! Second, it is an obstacle to God's work in and though his people to insist that the ways we used to minister were good enough in the past, so they should be good enough now and into the future.

Do you know the seven most deadly words to any ministry? *We've never done it that way before.* These words and the philosophy behind them have been a momentum killer in ministry throughout our movement—a movement that was once marked by Spirit-filled, risk-taking, and tradition-breaking come-outers!

To say that a challenge to tradition is ungodly and an affront to the saints of old only serves to expose our ignorance of the Word of God and our true Church of God heritage. Let's look briefly to the Word of God and our history for solutions. As we do so, I pray that we will find insights that will force a few of us to challenge our traditionalism and respond with resolute action.

Solution One: We should stop living in the good ol' days! Why? Because the Word of God tells us to do so. "Do not say, 'Why were the old days better than these?' For it is not wise to ask such questions" (Eccl 7:10). How then can we continue doing so? Is not this kind of thinking an affront to the eternal sense of creative newness that is the essence of the Holy Spirit of God, the Spirit that expresses himself in and through his children, the Church? What of this sense of newness?

Biblical theology is the theology of the new. Take a few minutes and look into the Word of God concerning this sense of what's new in the Spirit of God. (See Ps 40:3, 98:1; Eccl 1:9 brings balance; Isa 42:9, 62:2, 65:17, 66:2; Jer 31:31; Lam 3:23; Ezr 11:19, 18:31, 36:26; Zeph 3:5; Matt 9:17; Mark 16:17; Luke 5:39, 22:20; John 13:34; Acts 5:20; Rom 6:4; 1 Cor 5:7, 11:25; 2 Cor 3:6, 5:17; Gal 6:15; Eph 4:23–24; Col 3:10; Heb 8:8, 9:15, 10:20, 12:24; 1 Peter 1:3; 2 Peter 3:13; 1 John 2:8; Rev 2:17, 3:12, 21:1.)

In the interest of fairness, do the same concerning the Scriptures' exhortations for us to return to what is old. Having trouble finding it? Me, too! Apart from declaring that God exists "from of old" (Mal 5:2), even before there was a sense of time, the Bible places far less emphasis on the old. Isaiah 46:9 encourages us, "Remember the former things, those of long ago; I am God, and there is no other; I am God, and there is none like me." I would suggest that there are ways of staying connected to our past without being bound to it. We may even use the past as a tool for staying future focused.

Solution Two: We should understand our historical roots. In my present and past pastorates, I have initiated an event called Heritage Sunday. On this day, we celebrate the wonderful heritage and history of the Church of God reformation movement. In the worship center, the stage is set with tangible reminders of our past. Pictures, books, videos, and music all focus our attention on our movement's beginnings. We make available numerous resources for further study into our humble beginnings. Of course, this is not truly a one-time event; we are proud to stay connected with our heritage at every turn. However, this annual event helps us "remember the former things," while not compromising the power of God in the present or the future.

Recently, I began a series of sermons on divine healing and spiritual deliverance. I began the series with the cry, "Extra! Extra! Read all about it! Miracle worker heals the lame, raises the dead, mighty works abound!" I then referred to copies of the *National Labor Tribune* from April 7, 1921, which we had made available on every seat. The front page of this paper was dedicated to a story about our own E. E. Byrum and his divine-healing meetings. Its bold type read, "Author of Great Works on Divine Healing, Phenomenal Evidence Shown." I went on to share about our strong history of belief in divine healing, in keeping with that of the New Testament church.

Getting back to our roots involves more than any single event. There must be at our core a philosophy of radical ministry that John W. V. Smith explains well:

The Church of God reformation represents what may be called a radical approach to the Christian faith. The pioneers were not at all ashamed to be called radical. Indeed, the early issues of the *Gospel Trumpet* carried the following descriptive slogan in the masthead: A Definite, Radical, Non-Sectarian Journal. However, these leaders did not mean that they were choosing to be extremists or fanatics. Far from it. They abhorred fanaticism and were careful to keep from being identified with extremists. By radicalism these people meant simply that they were seeking to restore the true ideals of Christianity as it was set forth in the New Testament.[1]

We must see ourselves again as radicals! However, this time we need to rebel not against denominational and sectarian Babylon, but against our own nondenominational, self-sanctified devotion to the same old, same old.

The battles Jesus waged in his ministry were so often fought on the grounds of traditionalism. Did he not chastise the Pharisees and teachers of the law, saying, "Thus you nullify the word of God for the sake of your tradition"? (Matt 15:6). Now I am certainly not claiming that our present state as a movement is pharisaical. But I would suggest that we are in no danger, in just about any corner of our movement, of being too radical, on the cutting edge, or the first to "boldly go where no man has gone before."

Another characteristic pervading our movement today that is foreign to our movement's pioneers—in their brush harbor meetings, impromptu storefront meetings, and barn revivals—is a sense of formalism. They had respect, yes. They had a reputation for doing "all things decently and in order" (1 Cor 14:40), of course. But did they have an air of formality, too easily confused with self-righteousness and pseudo-piety? Never. The formality I have witnessed as I have traveled in the ministry of song and the Word throughout our movement is not

---

1. John W. V. Smith, *A Brief History of the Church of God Reformation Movement* (Anderson, IN: Warner Press, 1956), 25.

a testimony to the freedom we claim to possess, but to the bondage we are supposed to have fled. What is the solution for this? D. L. Moody speaks to this much better than I could hope to do when he asserts,

> The next thing the Spirit of God does is to give us liberty. He first imparts love; He next inspires hope, and then gives liberty, and that is about the last thing we have in a good many of our churches at the present day. And I am sorry to say there must be a funeral in a good many churches before there is much work done, we shall have to bury the formalism so deep that it will never have any resurrection. The last thing to be found in many a church is liberty.[2]

One of our choruses further describes what my heart is struggling to explain:

> Spirit of the living God, fall fresh on me
> Melt me, mold me, fill me, use me.
> Spirit of the living God, fall fresh on me.[3]

Do we mean it? Is the Spirit free to fall upon us in the middle of one of our carefully choreographed and sequentially programmed services or tediously timed small group meetings? I am simply longing for the Spirit's freedom to move throughout our movement in a way that it is not so much the exception anymore. I know some of you share this yearning with me. Indeed, this was the longing of our movement's founders. Consider a piece shared by A. L. Byers, quoting D. W. M'Laughlin:

> The apostolic church fully recognized the personal presence and authority of the Holy Ghost. He was fully accepted as their teacher and guide. They fully embraced the words of Jesus: "When he, the Spirit of truth, is come, he will guide you into all truth" (John 16:13)—yea, "teach you all things" (John 14:26), even the "deep things" (1 Cor 2:10) of God.

---

2. D. L. Moody, *Secret Power* (Chicago: Fleming H. Revell, 1908), 26.

3. Daniel Iverson, "Spirit of the Living God," in *Worship the Lord: Hymnal of the Church of God* (Anderson, IN: Warner Press, 1989), 265.

Hence, we hear Peter saying unto Ananias, "Why hath Satan filled thine heart to lie to the Holy Ghost?" (Acts 5:3) The presence of the divine Spirit was to them a certainty.

In Acts 13:2 we read, "As they ministered to the Lord, and fasted, the Holy Ghost said, 'Separate me Barnabas and Saul for the work whereunto I have called them.'" Here the authority of the Holy Ghost is recognized. Thus we see that the early church needed no man-made system; being filled with the Holy Ghost they fully accepted him as their teacher and guide. But in process of time the church lost her primitive power; the presence of the Holy Ghost seemed less real....

Indeed the modern church has so far lost sight of the veritable presence and authority of the personal Holy Ghost, that everything seems reduced to man-ordered system—yea, an endless treadmill of works. The form of religion takes the place of vital godliness, and the people seem to have forgotten that there is any Holy Ghost.[4]

This is the message we have been given, the legacy handed down to us. It is a message of Holy Spirit freedom, not endless systems of bureaucracy. We need an organizational audit in every local church to answer the question, Is there any apostolic authority here? Or are we bound by a spiritualized democracy, board, committee, and majority rule?

Get together with your elders or church council and ask concerning your ministries, Is what we are doing traditional, biblical, both, or neither? Perhaps other questions will naturally flow, for instance, How long have we done it this way? Is there a better way, a different way? If we always do what we have done, will we always get what we have gotten? Has anyone gotten saved around here lately? If not, why not?

And then there's my favorite: So what are we going to do about it? (See James 1:22–25.)

---

4. Quoted in Andrew L. Byers, *Birth of a Reformation: Life and Labors of Daniel. S. Warner* (Anderson, IN: Gospel Trumpet Co., 1921), 309–10.

7.

Methodology Matters

For a man's ways are in full view of the Lord, and he examines all his paths. —Proverbs 5:21

> Gimme that old-time religion.
> Gimme that old-time religion.
> Gimme that old-time religion,
> It's good enough for me.
>
> It was good for Paul and Silas.
> It was good for Paul and Silas....
> (Traditional)

IS THIS a great example of doctrinal truth in song or one of those old favorites that we sing in spite of its lack of scriptural accuracy? If by "old-time religion" we refer to the New Testament theology of salvation, sanctification, Christian unity, and so on, then by all means give me a double dose of it. However, if by old-time religion we mean we want New Testament theology only so long as it is processed, packaged, and delivered in an old-fashioned way, then I believe this is one of the most dangerous songs I have ever heard the people of our movement sing.

Interestingly enough, this philosophy often finds application in our local ministries. We continue to do the same things we have always done, in the ways we have always done them. But when it comes to other areas of life, we say, "Give me the latest, greatest, and best, and the sooner the better!"

Let me give you a good example, using our methodology of vacations. Some folks still like to camp out—rough it—in the most primitive sense of the words. More power to you hearty souls! The rest of us want to be pampered. I recall a conversation I had recently with one of our state leaders who was lamenting the lack of funding and low attendance at state camp meeting. I suggested that, culturally, we might have passed the days of camp-style communal living. I asserted that even among RV and camping enthusiasts, vehicles and tents might better be described as mobile Taj Mahals. Further, I suggested that the lack of funding for state camp meeting was not a matter of money. That is, I disagreed with the assertion that there just wasn't enough money to hold camp meeting at a vacation resort or a modern hotel setting. This state leader asserted that our people and pastors (many of whom are bivocational, he reminded me) just couldn't afford such an endeavor. So I told him about a conversation I had at a recent ministers meeting.

We were enjoying a short break in the day of meetings and grabbed some coffee. "Did you like your trip?" one pastor asked a neighboring pastor.

"Yeah, Alaska is beautiful."

"Did you do any fishing while you were there?"

"No, but I would like to do that next time!"

"I couldn't believe the size of some of the glaciers," another chimed in, "and to think that they are even bigger under the surface! We are already planning our next visit. Several families from the church are going as well. We've done it for years!"

"Yeah," said another pastor. "We have been several times ourselves. We like it much better than the Caribbean, but the grandkids like the beach, so I guess that's where we will go next."

This coffee-break conversation was between several of our full-time and bivocational pastors of average and even small churches. On and on went the conversation. I just kind of tucked it away in my memory bank. Now please, don't get me wrong! These are fine Christian workers and I'm sure that they are most worthy of their salaries. I don't dispute the idea that their families deserve seasons of rest and relaxation. (My family and I are big cruise fans ourselves!) That is not the point. The point is, after the coffee break, we returned to yet another committee discussion of what we could do to see our state ministries grow. The discussion was quickly dominated by the perception that there are just not enough resources available. Pastors around the table recited all the reasons why we can't afford to (or just plain shouldn't) change our ways of doing ministry as a state.

My dear colleagues in ministry, I'm not buying it anymore! We should not buy into the old, tired perception of the poor church. The fact is, we are scarcely different than our secular counterparts in one respect: We will invest in what we have a passion for. You don't believe me? Then what of this assertion? "For where your treasure is, there your heart will be also" (Matt 6:21).

As real as this false perception of our beggarly financial resources is, the deeper problems of our ministry are not essentially money matters. I suggest that this is a smoke screen that obscures the real issue, methodology. We just don't like change! I believe we are infected with what might be called the Bronze Serpent Syndrome. I had the privilege of sharing my heart burden about this at the last National Credentials Congress held in Estes Park, Colorado, in the fall of 2003. That presentation comprises the rest of this chapter:

Alfred North Whitehead said that "the art of progress is to preserve order amid change and to preserve change amid order." May I submit that the future for the Church of God must lie, not solely in a reformation of doctrine and theology, but in a sweeping reformation of methodology? That is to say, we must learn to preserve that which we hold sacred through a time of profound change!

Read the story of Moses and the bronze serpent (Num 21), as well as the reference to this account in John 3:14–15. The problem of the bronze serpent is a lesson lost to the past and now to the present generation. We must learn this lesson again and again if we are to relate the gospel of Jesus Christ in its fullness. Take a look at 2 Kings 18:1–4:

> Now it came about in the third year of Hoshea, the son of Elah king of Israel, that Hezekiah the son of Ahaz king of Judah became king. He was twenty-five years old when he became king, and he reigned twenty-nine years in Jerusalem; and his mother's name was Abi the daughter of Zechariah. He did right in the sight of the Lord, according to all that

his father David had done. He removed the high places and broke down the sacred pillars and cut down the Asherah. He also broke in pieces the bronze serpent that Moses had made, for until those days the sons of Israel burned incense to it; and it was called Nehushtan. (NASB)

This is our sickness, our syndrome. We are a generation still gazing at the forms of our past glory, the images of our own bronze serpents that were once altogether Spirit-ordained tools of ministry. The anointing, the presence, and the power of God has long-since left them, yet we worship these forms and we teach others to do the same. We fashion poles of our personal preference on behalf of our people, put our bronze serpents on them, and teach our people to bow to them. Yes, they still have a form of godliness but deny the power thereof (2 Tim 3:5). We have been bitten by the serpent of nostalgia. We need the antidote and we need it fast.

The antidote is still the new wine of God's truth (Matt 9:17). Even if we could organize a nationwide inoculation drive, without the pure antidote, our snake-bitten generation would die a slow but sure death. Yes, the antidote (the new wine) is old, but also ever new. It is pure and plentiful and does not need to be watered down in order to be stretched farther or better tolerated by the masses.

I believe God's Spirit is still calling people who are seeking to be a part of something redemptive in our world. They know who they are, whose they are, what they believe, and why they believe it. That redemptive "something" is the Church of God reformation movement and that "who" is Jesus Christ, raised, not on a pole, but on a cross as the Savior of the world.

I would further assert that today's candidates for pastoral ministry need to know that they can grow powerful congregations without compromising doctrinal purity. They can passionately preach salvation, sanctification, and a consecrated life in the Holy Spirit, and still relate and be relevant to this and any future generation.

We are so unified on this point that I would love to just say amen and go home, but that is precisely the problem. We forget that this is only half of the solution. We seem to believe that merely preaching the truth is enough. We assume that the masses should be left to apply it to themselves. The second part of the solution is this: The new wine must be delivered in new wineskins, i.e., new methodologies (Matt 9:17). In order to do this, we must begin living in the future. Dr. Nathan Woods, a noted theologian of the Church of the Nazarene, is quoted as saying:

> The Future is the source. The Future is unseen, unknown, except as it continually embodies itself visible in the Present. The Present is what we see, and hear, and know. It is ceaselessly embodying the Future, day by day, hour by hour, and moment by moment. It is perpetually revealing the Future, hitherto invisible. The Future is logically first, but not chronologically. For the Present exists as long as Time exists, and was in the absolute beginning of Time. The Present has existed as long as Time has existed. Time acts through and in the Present. It makes itself visible only in the Present. The Future acts, and reveals itself, through the Present. It is through the Present that Time, that the Future, enters into union with human life. Time and humanity meet and unite in the Present. It is in the Present that Time, that the Future, becomes part of human life, and so is born and lives and dies in human life. The Past in turn comes from the Present. We cannot say that it embodies the Present. On the contrary Time in issuing from the Present into the Past becomes invisible again. The Past does not embody the Present. Rather it proceeds silently, endlessly, invisibly from it. The Present therefore comes out from the invisible Future. The Present perpetually and ever-newly embodies the Future in visible, audible, livable form; and returns again into invisible Time in the Past. The Past acts invisibly. It continually influences us with regard to the Present which we know, and with reference to the Future which we expect to see.[1]

---

1. Taken from *Communiqué* at http://www.communiquejournal.org/q4_random. html. Passage is attributed to Ray Stedman at http://www.pbc.org/dp/stedman/gems.

Are you with me? Do you get it? (Good, because I'm not even sure that I get it!) Yet this is is just how our message comes across to those seeking truth when we insist on packaging it in our ancient and almost hieroglyphic scripts and forms. Let me ask, how many of us are likely to face heart surgery in the future? Statistically speaking, quite a few of us are likely to need it. So how do you want your heart surgery to be performed? The way it was done thirty years ago? Or do you want the latest knowledge and the latest technology, applied by men and women who are trained in that knowledge and technology?

There need not be any conflict, divisiveness, and disunity in the movement on this point. If we get our old-fashioned, self-sanctified methodologies off our homemade poles of personal preference, we may be able to fix the present and coming generation's eyes on Jesus Christ instead. It comes down to this: new wine can be preserved and delivered only in new wineskins, yet we still try to convince ourselves that the wineskins (that is, our methods) are not important, only the purity of our doctrine.

Let me give another illustration. Ever since George Mallory and Andy Irvine made their ill-fated attempt at the summit of Mount Everest in 1924, adventurers have been enlisting Sherpas (expert native guides) in their efforts to scale that rock of rocks. More and more climbers have succeeded as time has gone by, and both technology and technique have improved. In fact, many people have now reached the summit of Everest. Yes, some have died trying, but the success rate continues to grow. And with that success, a problem has developed. That majestic mountain, as well as other well-traveled mounts, have become dumping grounds. Used tools of the trade, such as empty oxygen bottles, food wrappers, discarded tent equipment, and other trash, now litter both the traditional campsites and the points in between. Now new expeditions are scaling the heights, but not for the glory of reaching the summit. No, they are risking their lives on Mount Everest to collect garbage! Expeditions to bring down refuse from the summit are being scheduled with increased frequency. Such trash not only mars one of the most majestic places on earth, but it makes new attempts at the summit much more difficult as adventurers come upon old tools of the trade and are tempted to use them, or subject themselves to further risk by having to go around them.

My point is simply this: People are trying to ascend higher and higher, pressing toward the summit of the Rock of Jesus Christ. But our trash and tools of the trade are strewn carelessly all over the Mountain of God. My fellow sherpas, we have some cleaning up to do if future expeditions are to reach the summit safely without being confused, thrown off course, or endangered by the used-up tools we have left behind.

Perhaps we also need to revive the spirit of Hezekiah, who wasn't afraid to do the most loving thing he could have done for his generation by breaking some poles and smashing some man-made idols. Pastor Bill Hybels says:

> Sadly, most local churches are functioning at only a fraction of their redemptive potential. Too often, visions are fuzzy, values are undefined, and volunteers are unmotivated. Revitalizing defeated churches is a huge challenge. Turning around a Fortune 500 corporation would likely extract less blood from a leader. (That's why this book is so terribly important.) As we move into the twenty-first century, massive changes must be made in how we do church. Yesterday's approaches will not work tomorrow. We must learn not only what to improve, but how to make the transitions manageable. In other words, how can we remedy the flock's illness without making it sicker? God is going to have to raise up a whole new generation of church leaders who see themselves more as change agents than maintainers; pioneers instead of pacifiers.[2]

I believe in the Church of God reformation movement! I believe the future is full of promise. My prayer is that we can raise up a new

---

2. Bill Hybels, introduction to *How to Change Your Church (without Killing It)*, by Alan Nelson and Gene Appel (Nashville, TN: W Publishing, 2000).

generation that is trained in both new wine and new wineskins, a generation that will have the courage to destroy the bronze serpents that plague so many of us. Before closing this chapter, let me share another great quote from *How to Change Your Church (without Killing It)*:

> What would happen if thousands of churches had a love for lost people so great that they would be willing to obey whatever God led them to do to communicate his love in ways that people could grasp, accept, and grow in? Imagine what would happen in your church if you and other key leaders were willing to change anything except the unchanging message of the gospel in order to build bridges in your community... While Jesus Christ is the same yesterday and today and forever (Heb 13:8), the message endures, but the methods must adapt. While the apostle Paul wrote his books with a quill and papyrus, we are using laptop computers with e-mail and laser printers. Paul shouted above the noise of the marketplace. We use cordless lapel microphones. He wore a toga. Aren't you glad we don't? Same message; different culture. Different times call for different methods.[3]

I say, amen to that! May we get over our petty personal preferences, our stubborn insistence that things be done as we have always done them, and ourselves. May we learn to communicate the gospel in every Spirit-led way possible as we reach the lost for Jesus Christ.

---

3. Alan Nelson and Gene Appel, *How to Change Your Church (without Killing It)* (Nashville, TN: W Publishing, 2000): 8–9.

8.

Where Would Jesus Hold Camp Meeting?

ONLY WHEN we worship together on the other side of eternity will we realize the blessing that camp meetings have been to the people of God in North America. From the Church of God reformation movement and other holiness groups like it, to mainline denominations, independent churches, and missionary groups, camp meetings have served to unite the people of God like no other event for more than two centuries. Untold scores of people have been saved, sanctified, healed, delivered, called, and equipped by the Spirit of God in a camp meeting or camp experience. Whether the meeting was held indoors, outdoors, open-air, in a tent, a barn, or metal building, it has scarcely mattered to God's people. Certainly in the nineteenth and early twentieth centuries, people would come to camp meetings in droves. Distance was hardly a concern. Hard travel was given, even if it meant traveling for days. The people's only lament was the inevitable fact that, all too soon, camp meeting would come to a close for another year. Without question, God used camp meetings as a foundation for evangelical Christianity in North America. It could be well argued that whatever fruits of success and influence that North American Christians have borne in well over two centuries of ministry are owed in no small measure to the shared experience of old-fashioned camp meetings.

With this in mind, perhaps we should consider a few thought-provoking questions, and one in particular. Has the movement of God that once filled these edge-of-town, out-of-the-way, and sometimes makeshift camps with eager worshippers and hungry disciples now left the camp meeting experience and their beloved facilities altogether? Has the Spirit of God simply moved on to other things? Has there been a deliberate, divine change of course in order to reach a changing culture through those still willing to follow his lead? Might there be a better way to accomplish the same purposes fulfilled so well by meetings and events of old? And are there even greater purposes yet unfulfilled?

Would it be appropriate to suggest that what made camp meetings such a treasured tradition never had much to do with the locations—the fields, hills or hollows, old tents, barns, clapboard buildings, or metal structures? Our best sense of sacred tradition, of what is now fast becoming a forlorn and even mourned nostalgia, would seek to convince us otherwise. Such a question deserves at least passing consideration if we truly are interested in how God would propel us into the future. I believe we can be sure of this: What camp meeting was at the zenith of its glory days, and what it represented at its saving and healing best, was never bound to its location. Rather, it was inextricably bound to the Spirit of God moving in and through his people.

One more question may help us come to terms with the place of camp meeting in the modern Christian culture, and especially the movement known as the Church of God: Where would Jesus hold camp meetings? To answer this question, we might consider the character of Christ, his calling to ministry, and some of the methodologies he used in ministering to the masses. Perhaps we can find direction more readily by focusing on Christ's example in ministry rather than seeking to trace the history of camp meeting as the validation for its own existence. Tracing the history of camp meetings would only bring to the table as many subjective perspectives and differing experiences as there have been camp meeting faithful. No, the only constant we have by which to measure our ministry is Christ and what Scripture reveals from his life and ministry as a model for ours.

Certainly, we could list the fruits of the Spirit as recorded in Galatians 5 as a fitting description of Christ's character. However, is there one word that would serve to summarize all of these as a reflection of the fruits displayed in his ministry? *Compassion* may be that word. Christ's compassion was full of all of the spiritual fruits, abounding in measure according to each need and each occasion.

If we attempted to recite all of the examples of Christ's compassion recorded in the Gospels, of course, we would have to insert almost the entirety of the Gospels themselves. So let's consider just one passage, Mark 6:34: "When Jesus landed and saw a large crowd, he had compassion on them, because they were like sheep without a shepherd." A more thorough reading of this chapter reveals that his compassion quickly turned the disciples toward action, resulting in the feeding of the crowd, both spiritually and physically. Compassion was Christ's divine response to the heartbeat of his Father, and our hearts should beat in time with his.

From Jesus' character came his calling. This point also requires little elaboration, and one passage could well represent the core of his calling. Luke 5:31–32 records Jesus' response to a religious leader's assertion that his ministry to the sinners of his day was misplaced: "It is not the healthy who need a doctor, but the sick. I have not come to call the righteous, but sinners to repentance." Jesus' calling was to seek and save the lost, the sinners, the seekers, and all those by any other name without his saving grace.

What then of Jesus' methodology, the purposed plans he set in motion to accomplish his divine ends as a culmination of both his character and calling? At this point we will insert our question for the day, Where would Jesus hold camp meeting?

If Jesus was concerned only with the schooling of his disciples, any place would do. As a matter of fact, getting away from the masses would serve this purpose more readily than attempting to do so in the marketplaces, town squares, or bustling neighborhoods—if that were even possible. Jesus chose more intimate and out-of-the-way settings for just this reason. American camp meetings have reflected this strategy, accomplishing the stated purpose of Christian unity and renewal, teaching the Word, and in many cases, fanning the flames for revival! But among what people and for what purpose?

It can be argued that Jesus sometimes did meet with the masses in the same type of out-of-town settings that most of our traditional camp meetings have used. But that was a strategic practicality. The crowds that began to follow Jesus from small village to bustling city simply could not be gathered around him right where he found them, especially as his ministry gained momentum. Jesus and his disciples had to find bigger and better venues in which to share the gospel. The Coliseum was simply not available to them. Nor was the local gymnasium or any other public venue, for that matter—not for radicals such as they. Some may debate this point, but it's less debatable that Jesus met people at the place and time of their need, regardless of where that took his ministry. Jesus went where the people were—not the religious people, but the ordinary people in all of their lostness—in order that they might be saved (Luke 19:10).

What if revival did break out in any one of our traditional camp-meeting settings? What influence and witness would that have in the world? Of course, this has occurred on countless occasions. We've seen great and momentous revival among the saints, where everyone is repenting and renewing, singing and shouting, prophesying and promising. We have seen "joy unspeakable and full of glory" on many occasions. But most often, something gets lost on the way back to town. Some of the fervor dies in recounting the experience to the saints back at the home church. The embers of the fires of Pentecost begin to fade the closer and closer we get back to the masses shivering in the cold of spiritual death.

Consider another approach. What if our annual camp meetings were held in the public forums provided in even some of the smallest burgs and hamlets? What if our heritage sings, our praise and worship gatherings, our sacred concerts, and our evangelistic services—including the preaching, teaching, healing, and wondrous seasons of fellowship—were held in full view of a whole village, town, city, or metropolis? (We could still call it a camp meeting if you wish, or a convention, a conference, or crusade. It hardly matters!) Then just imagine if God showed up and revival broke loose? Then it would happen right among (and perhaps even in) the very ones for whom we are given the very character and calling of Christ. Praise the Lord! What exposure this would give to the kingdom of God! What an influence it would exert in the local culture! What a witness to the community this could be!

Surely a husband is proud to be seen with his bride, especially in the public square.

This is largely lost when we meet in faraway places, segregated from the world in our safe places of refuge and retreat. We must ask ourselves, for what reason do we want revival? For our own renewal? Yes. For our own spiritual instruction? Of course. But revival has never been and must not be only for the sake of the redeemed.

Remember why Jesus did not allow his disciples to send the masses back to town to be fed (Mark 6:30–44). It wasn't so he could merely show off his miraculous powers. No, it was so that he could meet them right then, right there, right where they were, without sending them away. Our problem in the twenty-first century church is this: the masses just aren't following us out to the fields and hills and lakeshores like they did years ago—not unless there happens to be a hotel, a Starbucks, and a Wal-Mart nearby for their convenience. We can cry foul all we want. The cultural reality is what it is, however much we protest or wish it otherwise. This is the reality of our culture and we must be honest with ourselves. Besides, we haven't exactly been in revolt concerning these realities ourselves. Very, very few of us are lining up to book the cabins, camper spaces, or lodge rooms at our state campgrounds for our personal vacations or retreats, and deep down we all know why: we love and even depend on the creature comforts to which we have become accustomed.

I believe that Jesus still comes to our camp meetings today, regardless of their mostly out-of-the-way locations. However, I picture him sitting on the back row, perhaps leaning against a tent-pole near the exit or peering in through a side window. I think he is more than just a little distracted as he casts a longing gaze across the gravel lot, the neighboring field, over the hills, down the road, and into the busy streets of the nearest town or city, where all of his lost sheep are running about, most not even knowing they are without a shepherd. The songs of Zion cannot be heard at such distances. The lost do not hear our testimonies, prayers, teachings, and sermons. These good things are shared largely, sometimes exclusively, by those who are already found.

The mere thought of changing the beloved tradition of camp meeting is painful for many of us, yet one final consideration simply must be made. Scripture says this consideration will clearly indicate the passion of our hearts as God's people in the twenty-first century: "For where your treasure is, there will your heart be also" (Matt 6:21). We may beg to differ, offer vehement protest, or simply refuse to face the facts, but let's talk money. It's the heart of the matter, if you will.

I recently received a promotional brochure from one of our fine state ministries that was seeking funds for its evangelism board. "We need you!" the brochure said. It went on to implore each member of each congregation in the state to give just one dollar toward church restarts and planting. This is commendable. It's a step in the right direction. It is truly the Spirit's leadership.

But when viewed from another angle, the mere fact that evangelism is seen as a nonbudgeted ministry that must subsequently be funded with such promotions in this state is shameful. The upkeep and maintenance of our facilities receive priority or designated budget status, but evangelism is given discretionary status at best.

The ministry budgets in far too many districts and states reveal that our bottom line quite simply is not souls—at least not reaching the lost through evangelistic training and subsequent initiatives, strategic church planting, leadership renewal, and equipping. "But we believe in evangelism!" you protest. Yes, everyone's heart is in the right place. But while the just shall indeed live by faith, the world takes cash.

What am I getting at here? We spend, in some cases, more than fifty percent of our Kingdom dollars in district and state budgets on the maintenance of our camps and other physical facilities, which serve us (let alone the lost) less than fifty percent of the calendar year. That comes with complaints about camp conditions and subsequent requests for increasing the facilities budget every other year. Conversely, most district and state budgets allocate less than ten percent to evangelism and outreach, church planting, and so on. God truly help us! Church plants are dying on the vine and their planters with them. Local congregations are just trying to break even. Missionaries are struggling to make ends meet. Mission projects at home and abroad are often scarcely funded. But our old tabernacle got a major facelift this year and we built two more cabins! We can certainly continue to argue that evangelism and outreach are precisely what our campgrounds and camp meetings are for. But again, when the majority of our campgrounds are located in the out-of-the-way places, the world is just not coming. Although we used to be annually revived at our favorite camp-meeting event, we ourselves are scarcely going. At the same time, conferences at hotels, resorts, convention, and conference centers are sold out and must be booked well in advance—not merely for secular interests, but for an increasing variety of gatherings of God's people.

Nonetheless, at some point in every annual General Assembly meeting, folks will gather under that same old tree or in the dining hall over coffee and cookies to mourn the attendance of yester-year, saying, "People sure don't come to camp meeting like they used to." We just don't seem able to connect the dots. Regrettably, we will have some of the same conversations again next year.

Granted, our camps continue to serve well as places of retreat for small groups and are still great for the ongoing ministry of children's and youth camps. Many will pose very persuasive arguments on this point and cry, "Save the camps! Save our children!" Further, they insist that some of the following considerations more than justify the fact that we spend far more on inreach than outreach. They ask, "What about all those who were called into the ministry at that children's camp, youth camp, or camp meeting? What about all of those who are still being led in discipleship there today? And what about the wondrous fellowship we have enjoyed there? What of those who serve within these camp ministries?"

Praise the Lord! But shouldn't we at least consider whether there might be more viable contexts for such divine events? Is the Holy Spirit locality challenged? Could we not rent campgrounds from others for our annual events—and leave them with all of the overhead and up-keep expense for the rest of the year? Cannot people be faithfully called and led into discipleship, enjoy fellowship and find significant ministry in other locations just as well? Would the end of a camping program release some funds for modern evangelism? Why not entertain these arguments? Why not put them to rest once and for all, if they hold no validity?

Of course, some of us do not even use youth and children's camps as justification for the inordinate amount of money we spend on year-round camp ground facilities instead of investing in comprehensive outreach. We somehow feel fully justified in maintaining the state's annual budget percentages simply to keep a sacred event or two exactly as they have traditionally been, regardless of the alarming realities concerning our failing influence for Christ in North America. Some may also argue that other church groups have sold properties and facilities to limit overhead and save a buck for the Kingdom, but they did not increase their outreach to the lost or the planting healthy churches. Numerous reasons for those failures may exist, none of which should discount the wisdom of considering a change of course.

Perhaps you recall one of the classic definitions of insanity. It's doing the same thing over and over but expecting different results. We are spending more and more on inreach and precious little on outreach, yet we just can't seem to understand why we aren't growing. We will be held accountable.

Some will seek to argue doctrinally at this point. They believe that the decline in North America has little to do with our investment of Kingdom dollars. Rather, that this is just what the Bible predicts in the last days: few coming to salvation and many being deceived and falling. If this is a valid argument, then take it to its logical extreme. Why preach about the sanctification of saints any more than seeking of sinners, since these last days are obviously so predisposed toward doom and gloom, with even the very elect falling from grace?

Consider prayerfully for just a moment that the arguments to continue down the present path, to uphold our long-held traditions, may be based on sentimental reasons more than theological ones. In transactions of the soul, the physical location has a very vital, yet limited, role, whether it is the backwoods or a cutting edge conference facility. The final transaction is made in the soul, not any earthly sanctuary or facility. However, to the extent that facilities help us in seeking and saving those not yet found, would we not be better served with an environment that is more conducive to what we are trying to do?

And what if we had the Kingdom dollars for all the above? What if we could have our cake and eat it too? Oh, that our investment permitted such a luxury! However, I believe this would only mean that we had even more funds to funnel toward reaching the lost and not for continued upkeep of facilities that someday will be burned with a fervent heat. In the light of Jesus' character and calling, this discrepancy in stewardship may be more than just a problem for the twenty-first-century church to solve; it may be a corporate sin that we need to confess and repent of. Can we at least reason these points together?

O Church of God, I agree that we desperately need to come together for worship, fellowship, and discerning discourse. That has been our tradition every year in every district, every state, and on the national and global levels as well. Our unity is too important to neglect the assembling of ourselves together. Truly, God has moved mightily in these annual events. Again, perhaps therein lies part of the problem: our most significant gatherings are not designed to seek the lost, but merely to satisfy the sanctified and bring respite to the redeemed. If we insist that camp meetings prepare us to reach the lost, then where is the fruit of these efforts?

Perhaps the time has come to reconsider our methodologies of providing for both saint and sinner in a way that reflects the character, the calling, and heart of our Lord and Savior. The debates may be (perhaps need to be) intense, but something has got to give. Our statistics reveal a reality that we cannot ignore. Maybe we should come together in prayer and fasting for open, frank, and honest discourse concerning our past and present methodologies. Maybe we need to honestly ask ourselves, Where would Jesus hold camp meeting?

9.

Isolationism

I have other sheep that are not of this sheep pen. I must bring them in also. They too will listen to my voice, and there shall be one flock and one shepherd. —*John 10:16*

MOST OF US in the Church of God have come out and are plenty separate from the rest of the world. We are in little danger of contamination by "sect Babylon." Unfortunately, we may have come so far out that we are out of touch, not with the sinful world, but with what the Spirit of God is doing, both at home and abroad. I would assert that in our attempt to be the sanctified Church of God, we have sometimes lost touch with the larger world of the people of God. You do believe that at least some of the Baptists, Methodists, Assemblies of God, Christian Church people, and even Catholics have more than a decent chance of sharing in our eternal reward, don't you?

Sure, we have some distinct differences from other Christian groups, both doctrinally and methodologically. But please tell me that our anti-sectarianism hasn't led us as a movement to some deluded, even cultish belief that we are *the* chosen remnant alone, the only true sheep of the Shepherd!

Do I believe that our emphasis on sanctification, unity, and eschatology is biblically sound and relevant to a vital Christian experience? Yes, yes, and yes. But I also believe that God has, is, and will continue to use the greater church of God by his grace and for his glory as his return hastens towards us. I believe that includes people in all of the groups listed above, in addition to many other denomination, movements, and associations. No, I am not advocating a blind ecumenicalism. But I am saying that God is using the Church of God movement as a part of his greater plan *in spite of our faults*, and we ought to be mighty grateful that he continues to do so.

Dr. Gilbert Stafford addresses this issue well in his book, *Vision for the Church of God at the Crossroads*. In chapter eleven, "Living Out the Vision," he speaks about our tendency toward an arrogant isolationism:

> I had just finished presenting the historic vision of the Church of God to an ecumenical gathering made up of a wide spectrum of Christian traditions. From the looks on the faces of those listening to me, I sensed great appreciation for what I had said and was ready to entertain questions that would give me additional opportunity to expand the vision that I take delight in introducing to others. The first to speak, however, did not have a question but a comment. He said, "What you have shared with us is very commendable and I personally find it to be a beautiful vision. However, as I listened to you I found it difficult to put it together with one of your congregations not far from where I minister. The people in that church are rigid, resistant to any association with the rest of us, and rude when we try to make contact with them. The general consensus in our town is that the people in that church simply do not want to have anything to do with the rest of us and that they are quite happy doing their own thing. So we leave them alone."[1]

Ouch! Does this comment describe our movement as a whole? No, I don't think so. But do our beliefs leave us open to the temptation to overestimate ourselves in relation to other people of God? I'm afraid they do. (See Phil 2:1–11.)

The essential cure for isolationism is the spiritual fruit of humility. You see, the cousin of the original sin (pride) is arrogance, and arrogance is so often the driving force of isolation. We just feel like we don't need anyone's help or suggestions. After all, the "evening light"

---

1. Gilbert Stafford, *Vision for the Church of God at the Crossroads* (Anderson, IN: Warner Press, 2002), 100.

is most certainly shining with the greatest intensity through the lens of the Church of God, Anderson, Indiana! Right? I wish. I honestly, truly wish this were true...but it is not. Make no mistake, we have the right message, but our lens has been scratched and smudged, and it needs a little grinding and buffing to bring clarity once again. Enter humility. Merle D. Strege quotes early Church of God minister E. A. Reardon concerning unity:

> I am convinced that the gathering that God is most inter-ested in is our gathering unto Christ, and (that) there never will be one centralized and centrally-governed movement that will take in all the children of God on earth. There is no one place on earth from which God is directing all the affairs of his Kingdom and salvation work. There is no one body of people on earth who can claim an exclusive right to Christ and to all his light and truth. If Christ were here in person, he would certainly put to confusion those bodies of his professed followers who make themselves his exclusive people.... I cannot conceive of him as confining his opera-tions exclusively to this movement, and I am quite sure that the representative minds and spiritual hearts of our people do not hold such views.[2]

Let me suggest something a little more tangible in your local battle with isolationism, something that may be altogether unfamiliar to you. As a purposeful tool of vision and equipping of your church leaders, it's a tool that will certainly require a heavy dose of humility. It is called a vision quest. This is a trip specifically designed to inform and inspire your leadership. Simply find a vital church in your area or your re-gion, then contact their leadership and request a tour. Your visit should include not only a good look at their facilities (especially if you are considering your own building project) but perhaps a time of sharing with their leadership or an opportunity to attend one of their services or events. I cannot tell you how important this has been to our minis-

---

2. Merle D. Strege, *I Saw the Church* (Anderson, IN: Warner Press, 2002), 192.

try over the last few years. We have been informed concerning some very effective tools of ministry. We have learned even more as leader after leader, group after group has been gracious and humble enough to point out their mistakes and say, "Don't do this!" We have been inspired—the ooh and ahh factor has been very rewarding for us and has contributed to our own leadership vision.

Now we have pretty much covered our tri-state area concerning churches that are at the next level of growth, so what are we to do? We are going national. We are planning an annual trip to churches across North America to visit ministries such as the Brooklyn Tabernacle and the Times Square Church in New York City, Lakewood Church in Houston, Willow Creek Community Church in Chicago, and Saddleback Church in Southern California. Do we want to be just like these ministries? No. Do we agree with them on every point? Not at all. But we aren't going to throw the baby out with the bath water, either. We have much to learn about reaching this and future generations with the gospel of Jesus Christ. We can glean from others good examples of how to step out of our comfort zones and meet needs as never before.

In addition, I point my staff and lay leaders to other ministries' Web sites that offer some real food for thought. We call these cyber quests. Again, our objective is not to copy or imitate another ministry, but to be informed and inspired by their example.

We must know by now that we haven't arrived at perfection, but we share in the spirit of the apostle Paul when he said, "Though I am free and belong to no man, I make myself a slave to everyone, to win as many as possible. To the Jews I became like a Jew, to win the Jews...I have become all things to all men so that by all possible means I might save some" (1 Cor 9:19–22).

10.

Obstacles to Ministry Momentum

For in him we live and move and have our being. — Acts 17:28

"WE ARE ALL GOING or no one is going! After all, we believe in unity!" This philosophy represents a pseudo-unity that threatens to stop ministry momentum every time there is a mighty move of God. You see, what people are really saying is this: "If we don't all agree [and they often really mean, if everyone else doesn't agree with them], then we don't have unity. And if we're not unified, then it isn't right." They insist, "We love the church and just don't want to see anything bad happen." They may even purport to be the true guardians of the flock as they take their stand against the ministry leadership in all wisdom and holiness. On the surface, this sounds legitimate to the naïve. It seems to be said in a spirit of love, joy, peace, and longsuffering, so it must be right. Right? Not so fast.

I would suggest that far too many Spirit-filled leaders in local bodies have fasted and prayed, sought wise counsel, received direction from the Spirit, informed and equipped the church body, stepped out on faith, and seen some fruit as they began to plan and act upon a fresh vision, then failed to sustain the vision simply because they were afraid of losing even one individual or a couple of key families, let alone a group. "Forget about the direction of God, Jonah! The Joneses don't like it, so we aren't going to Nineveh!" Sadly, you and I know this routine well.

About every five years or so, a congregation grows—maybe even doubling in its size and scope of influence—then slides back as things get a little too uncomfortable for some tenaciously tenured parishioners. If the ministry leaders persist in the effort to move forward, then one way or another, there is a leadership change, and I'm not talking lay leadership! The change is made *for the good of the church.* The church then stalls for a couple years or so. (This is to be expected, the local folks reason.) Then they celebrate survival, muddle through, and eventually start all over again. Time and time and time again, the same sad story is told. Perhaps you think this story is a bit harsh, but please bear with me as I suggest a different perspective and some possible solutions to this sad state of affairs.

I submit that congregations who think this routine is to be expected or inevitable will, in truth, not grow or sustain spiritual momentum until they lose a few people. I suggest that if they truly love the church as they claim, then they will seek the whole counsel of the Word in defense of its health. They will find that the Word says a church's health is revealed through growth and maturation, and through bearing spiritual fruit, not the mere celebration of survival. To do so otherwise—to let the wind of the Spirit blow by without ever setting our sails—is just not an example of real love for God's church.

Let me qualify this. More times than not, love is involved in this mad cycle, but it is love for tradition, love for comfort, love for the status quo, and love for those in a holy huddle. Until those with a vision (especially the pastoral and lay leaders) accept the fact that some folks may not go with them through the transitions and the growing pains, then they are doomed to repeat this sad history time and again.

Am I saying that you can't make an omelet without breaking a few eggs? No, that would be cynical. We are in the people-building, not the people-breaking, business. However, let's take a scriptural look at the life of the church. Let's prayerfully discern the possibility of going to a higher level in ministry, even though not everybody may be going with us.

God gives direction to the church, chiefly through the pastoral and lay leadership. This is why God has given to the church "some to be apostles, some to be prophets, some to be evangelists, and some to be pastors and teachers" (Eph 4:11). If those tenaciously tenured critics really do know better than the leaders, then they should step up to assume church leadership with all of its responsibilities, rewards, and punishments. Until then, Scripture says, people of the congregation are to receive instruction and equipping from the leadership they have, and serve accordingly with a willing spirit.

Think about it: Did those who oppose to the new direction of ministry attend the prayer and planning meetings leading up to it? Were they privy to the many, many seasons of sharing concerning the direction of the ministry? If not, then how can they begin to know better than their leaders? And how can we keep from gently pointing this out? I know this course of action is often in conflict with the secularized leadership structure we have conveniently created in most congregations, which is a democratic form of majority rule. But this system reflects precious little of the apostolic, Spirit-led life of the church described in the New Testament. The local church is a theocracy, not a democracy. We operate by Spirit rule, not majority rule. And the Spirit unquestionably leads through spiritual leaders. Take one of Israel's first forays into majority rule, as recorded in Numbers 13–14 and Deuteronomy 1:26–36. The majority of the men who explored the Promised Land felt that they just couldn't take it or it just wasn't worth the risk! The result? They sentenced themselves and the rest of the nation to wander in the wilderness for forty years! Not one (except Joshua and Caleb) inhabited the Promised Land.

God does not direct us to retreat or fall victim to atrophy. No, in the face of difficulty his direction is at least to stand firm (Eph 6:13–14) while we wait for his clear call to march to spiritual war, or to go and grow, or to believe and build! "Enlarge the place of your tent, stretch your tent curtains wide, do not hold back; lengthen your cords, strengthen your stakes. For you will spread out to the right and to the left; your descendants will dispossess nations and settle in their desolate cities. Do not be afraid; you will not suffer shame. Do not fear disgrace, you will not be humiliated" (Isa 54:2–4). Have we Christians been given a Great Suggestion or a Great Commission? If any think that our marching orders are optional, let them opt out.

Just because everyone isn't going doesn't mean you shouldn't go! In fact, not everyone will go with you to the next level. God said through the prophet Jeremiah, "But I gave them this command: Obey me, and I will be your God and you will be my people. Walk in all the ways I command you, that it may go well with you. But they did not listen or pay attention; instead, they followed the stubborn inclinations of their evil hearts. They went backward, and not forward" (Jer 7:23–24). Example after example is given in Scripture of times when some of God's company did not want to move forward. Either they got with the program and went anyway, or they didn't...and suffered greatly for it.

It is okay to move obstacles (in the form of people) out of the way in order to facilitate the movement of God in and through his people. Remember this eyebrow raiser? Jesus turned and said to Peter, "Get behind me, Satan! You are a stumbling block to me; you do not have in mind the things of God, but the things of men" (Matt 16:23). The apostle Paul understood this principle as well. He knew that some people may hinder the work of the church because, no matter how religious they may be, they are not true brethren. "This matter arose because some false brothers had infiltrated our ranks to spy on the freedom we have in Christ Jesus and to make us slaves. We did not give in to them for a moment, so that the truth of the gospel might remain with you" (Gal 2:4–5).

And what of the sin of Achan (Josh 7)? He pursued his own selfish agenda, regardless of the devastating results to the rest of the army. In response, Joshua didn't make excuses for him or put his spin doctors into action to cover it all up. Nor did Joshua allow one family to keep the rest of God's people from fulfilling the call God had given them. To say the least, Achan and his family didn't go with them to the next destination.

Removing such human obstacles should be done carefully, prayerfully, and purposefully. By carefully, I mean that there should be a system or guide in place clearly reflecting the methodology and spirit of Matthew 18. (See also Chapter 11 concerning the use of covenants.) Our national, as well as most state, offices offer a variety of resources to help you achieve reconciliation and restoration, but not enough local bodies take advantage of the wise counsel offered.

The goal is always for restoration and revival to take place in the hearts and minds of all. This is our earnest prayer throughout a planned process of dealing with opposition to a church's leaders. Both restoration and revival are possible through the application of the Word and submission to the Holy Spirit's discipline and instruction.

By prayerfully, I mean doing something that I am confident is altogether foreign to most pastors. How about gathering your ministry leaders and praying a prayer I was taught several years ago—a prayer you may have never prayed before—concerning those who are coming against the vision God has given? Pray, "Lord, please move them up (in love, faith, unity, and understanding through confession and repentance) or move them out." Implementing any sort of church discipline may not be necessary if you are willing to pray for God to answer this prayer. We would always prefer that our critics do the former; we hope that many will indeed move up. However, it is no less a God thing if they move out. Further, to allow this kind of opposition or facilitate it is to join in killing the momentum that God has so graciously given! This would be a grievous sin because we are reminded that "anyone, then, who knows the good he ought to do and doesn't do it, sins" (James 4:17).

Finally, when I say that you should deal with such people obstacles purposefully, I mean to make up your mind that you are, in fact, moving forward, even if this means some will not be going with you. This was vital when we became partners with First Church of God in Ashland, Kentucky. I recall the most thorough candidacy process we had ever been through. Numerous phone calls, a conference call, a two-day sightseeing visit and fellowship, then a three-day weekend tryout were all accompanied by much prayer and fasting. During one of our weekend dinners, the church's lay leaders and I were speaking freely about our testimonies and philosophies of ministry when I asked a question: "So why haven't you grown like you say you have always wanted?" There was an immediate break in the *koinonia*, replaced by a spirit of restlessness and tension. The question was given the old end around by the vice chairman of the council, who also served as the chairperson of the pulpit committee.

I wasn't very satisfied with this response but was relieved when he pulled me aside later that evening to explain why he felt he had to deflect the direction of the conversation for the moment. He explained that a group of five or six families had been hard workers and faithful supporters over many years and always claimed to only want the best for the church, but they nevertheless made sure things went their way. They never wanted the church to go too far beyond what they were comfortable with and could carefully manage themselves. He even recounted occasions where ministry initiatives were agreed upon by the pastoral and lay leadership, but because these families weren't completely in favor (even though they may have voted in favor of it, so as not to be seen as the bad guys), the idea would just die a slow death or never materialize. This was the real order of things. No one dared to challenge these quiet coups of leadership. So, every time the ministry gained momentum and the congregation grew to around three hundred persons or so, this group would begin to question the direction things were heading. They put their feet on the brakes and began to work for a leadership change—not their leadership, of course, but the pastoral or lay leadership.

On hearing this, I forced the issue. I asked him two questions then and there. First, "Are some of these folks in leadership now?" (He responded yes to this question.) And second, "Are the rest of you willing to stand with me this time around, regardless of the reactions or actions of this group?" I assured him that, although I would seek to bring unity with this group in every way I knew how, I would not sacrifice the vision of this congregation upon the altar of their wills. For his part, he said yes to this question. However, unbeknown to me, he proceeded to check with other lay leaders and got their affirmation of support before the weekend was out. He said that they were tired of hitting the same wall over and over, only enjoying limited growth and manageable victories. They would stand with me against anyone who would stop or limit a vision to reach the lost for Christ, period. This assurance went a long way toward the decision my wife and I made to join with them in growing a ministry of regional influence and beyond. Was this trickery? Was it out of line? No, in defense of a vision for reaching the lost, we agreed it was akin to being "wise as a serpent and harmless as a dove" (Matt 10:16).

It is okay to say, "God bless you as you go," and then let those in opposition leave or even facilitate their going. Do not turn around and go after them. (See Rom 16:17–20 and Titus 3:9–11.) I am familiar with the argument and reasoning that Matthew 12 means, if everyone isn't going, no one is going! According to this interpretation, if anyone does go astray (code for slam on the brakes), then we must stop the bus, get off, and get them back, regardless of what it means to those still on board or to the travel established by the Great Driver of the ministry bus, just as it is picking up momentum.

I believe that Matthew 12 does describe believers who get a little confused and stray from the course, a little tired and fall behind, or tempted and fall away from the fellowship. But I don't believe the strays of Matthew 12 are people who make up their minds that they just don't like the shepherds or don't like the new pastures, and then tell all the other sheep about it. It's not about sheep who refuse to grow any more wool (or complain incessantly as they do), encourage other sheep to do the same, and threaten to leave the fold if they don't get their sheepish ways.

No, these ploys must be challenged out of a true love for the church and the lost who are waiting for us to come and get them! Yes, there may be times when some folks just don't understand the vision and need some additional, patient instruction. If this is the case, then go the extra mile. Take the time to instruct them. With a little extra attention and assurance, these folks will again be ready to go. And yes, it is possible that you may be trying to go a little too fast, but this does not mean that the direction itself is wrong or that moving forward at a steady pace isn't still the will of God, no matter what those in opposition may say. Be discerning. Then let those in willful opposition go with your blessing.

If you are following the Word and Spirit and are actually going somewhere, then you are going to lose some people. The question is, how many? In our

Ashland ministry, we lost about thirty people and gained over three hundred in the first three years. Now, I would like to lose absolutely no one whatsoever. However, that scarcely being an option, if I am moving in the Spirit, I can and will live with these numbers. One could argue, "But you lost over thirty people! How can you say that was part of God's will?" I hear you, but I would argue against this reasoning. The fact is, losing thirty people is better than losing over three hundred. Now, did I know about the three hundred when we lost the thirty? No, not in the flesh. Those three hundred had yet to appear, but we knew in our spiritual minds, saw with our spiritual eyes, and believed with spiritual hearts that they and many more were on the line if thirty people were allowed (once again!) to quench the Spirit and halt the momentum of God in a growing ministry. And I am quite sure that God saw those three hundred people well before we did.

I recall watching a documentary on the D-day invasion. This greatest of all military landings was agreed by most military experts to be a do-or-die mission. The very outcome of the war depended upon its success. The stakes were as high as they can get on this earth—freedom from the clutches of an insane dictator and his powerful war machine. I saw a film clip taken that very day aboard one of the ships. The men were clearly told that many of them would scarcely make it onto the beach. However, they knew that the time was now or never, and that the fate of their loved ones was truly at stake. Eventually, the enemy would come to every doorstep if not stopped now. The soldiers counted the cost, knew there would be grave loss, and deemed the goal worthy of it all. They may have wanted to spare their lives that day by just hoping that the worst could somehow be avoided, but they knew better. The stated objective of the enemy was clear. Thankfully, the battle was won by those brave men. As a result, millions and millions of people were set free.

If you are convinced that God has spoken to you and given you a vision, if he is now moving you according to that vision, then what are you saying, what are you doing if you allow anything to stop it? Talk about scary! I fear God too much to be party to this kind of double-minded second-guessing.

And what is really being said by those who stand against the movement of God, even though no one may actually voice it? They are saying this: "Even though you have prayed, fasted, received wise counsel, maybe already voted, ratified, and moved forward to begin realizing this vision, you haven't really heard from God at all. We are right and you are wrong. This has gone far enough. Therefore, we are not going any farther with you." What else could they possibly mean if not this? If they do not trust your leadership on this matter, how can they trust you on any other? How can they trust you to preach or teach or discern the will of God on matters of lesser or greater importance?

I have heard all of the rationales to pull back and do nothing. Yes, I am sure they really are nice folks. Of course, they don't mean to be difficult (nobody ever does). They have only the best interest of the flock at heart. Further, "They love you, Pastor (or lay leader), but not the direction you're taking us." But in the end, the rationales just don't matter. The movement of God is squelched, regardless of the reasons we give. Consider that most auto collisions are accidents where no one meant to collide, but tell that to those who were injured or to families who lost a loved one. It is scarcely a word of solace. The damage was done, regardless of the intent of those involved.

This is a hard lesson to learn and even harder to apply. However, it manifests love for the family of God in a deeper way than many of us have ever realized. Yes, restoration—getting people to get with the program as the Spirit leads—is our ultimate goal. But when some refuse to do so and they take a stand against what God is doing, don't give in. Don't sacrifice the vision of God. Don't forget to count all of those you are likely to lose if you *don't* move forward. Begin to pray, "Lord, move them up, or move them out." Then, love the flock enough to facilitate this as the Spirit and Word give further orders.

11.

Reckless Autonomy

Be careful, however, that the exercise of your freedom does not become a stumbling block to the weak. —1 Corinthians 8:9

THIS CHAPTER will be longer than the rest. However, its length is necessary to explain a concept that sadly has been lost as a ministry methodology.

Recall the state of God's chosen people as recorded in Judges 17:6, "In those days Israel had no king; everyone did as he saw fit." The covenants of old were compromised. The Israelites were fitting right in with a culture that was self-absorbed and self-assured. Moral relativism was the order of the day. The concept of personal accountability was all but lost to that wayward generation of God's people. Could this be the plight of far too many local, district, or national bodies of the Church of God? This is certainly worth considering.

Congregational autonomy itself is not to blame; it is certainly one of things so right about the Church of God. To be able to seek the face of God, discern his holy will and way, and reason together as the family of God at all levels, free of undue hierarchy and with only limited bureaucracy is no small part of the miracle that is the Church of God.

> No earthly master do we know, to man-rule will not bow,
> But to each other and to God eternal trueness vow.[1]

To be sure, autonomy is one of our greatest blessings. However, the slow but sure erosion of biblical accountability over the last fifty years has caused this blessing to become a potential curse, a stumbling block that we have laid in our own path. The general director of Church of

---

1. Charles W. Naylor, "The Church's Jubilee," in *Worship the Lord: Hymnal of the Church of God* (Anderson, IN: Warner Press, 1989), 312.

God Ministries, Dr. Ronald V. Duncan, has commented well concerning our autonomy and the continual challenge it presents:

> In recent years within the Church of God movement, the role of autonomy in the life of the church has been discussed in many venues. Autonomy has been blamed for many problems in the church, yet praised for providing congregational independence from national structures...Ultimately, balancing autonomy and body responsibility requires a blending of independence and dependence to produce interdependence. Too much of either one is unhealthy for the body of the redeemed. We really do need each other."[2]

I would submit that in the place of true scriptural accountability is now found a deceptively disguised individualism that wars against our true unity and fellowship in the Spirit. I wish to suggest a possible solution, a concept that can find ready application at all levels and perhaps bring about a degree of accountability that has been lost in our generation. That concept is called covenant ministry.

We have always needed a little help—no, a lot of help—with keeping our end of the bargain with God, specifically concerning obedience to his commands. To this end, God has graciously given his people something tangible each time he established a covenant with them to serve as a reminder of that relationship. Whether it was Noah's rainbow, Abraham's firepot and blazing torch, Moses' stone tablets, the spear of Phinehas, Nathan's revelation to David, or the very cross and empty tomb of Christ, God has given us something tangible to remind us of our mutual commitment. These reminders lend to us a sense of sobriety and sincerity, and we feel compelled by his Spirit to confirm our commitment in and through an obedient life. Although no Christian would dispute the essential role of the Holy Spirit in and through an obedient life, few now see the need for any further reminder of the commitment we have made. We somehow fancy ourselves above the need for this, which was so important to our predecessors in ministry.

---

2. Ronald V. Duncan, FRONTline, *ONEvoice!* magazine, no. 3 (2004): 4.

We feel we have the authority to do as we please, based on our God-given autonomy, and are quite confident this is enough to justify any means to our ends.

We know well the rules of our ministries; after all, we probably made them up ourselves. We suppose the Word of God is sufficient enough to keep us accountable to God and each other in a united sense of direction. But our record suggests that this simply is not the case. Increasing numbers of individuals, ministers, agency leaders, local bodies, districts, states, and national ministries just do their own thing with little regard for the consequences to the Kingdom, all the while waving the banner of the Church of God. Our unchecked sense of autonomy has given us the mentality of a sheriff in the old West who says, "I'm the law around these parts. Don't no one mess with the law." We contend that the Spirit and the Word are more than enough to keep us accountable, keep our individual heads out of the clouds, and keep our united hands to the plow. But have they been enough? Is more needed?

Some may ask, "More than the Spirit and Word?" Yes, but in the best sense of the Word itself and in keeping with the very work of the Spirit. Consider that Jesus often used an object lesson to lend realism to the divine point he was making. The very presence of the Holy Spirit on the day of Pentecost was accompanied by tangible phenomena—rushing wind and tongues of fire. These tangible things represented the spiritual work that was occurring. My point is this: no matter how spiritual we are, we need tangible forms and workable tools of accountability.

"I now establish my covenant with you and with your descendants after you and with every living creature that was with you—the birds, the livestock, and all the wild animals, all those that came out of the ark with you—every living creature on earth. I establish my covenant with you" (Gen 9:9–11). With these words to Noah, God set forth a method of accountability that would be the foundation upon which all subsequent, solid, and truly sanctified relationships would be built. Many covenants would follow: the covenant of Abraham (Gen 15:9–21; 17), the covenant at Sinai (Ex 19–24), the covenant of Phinehas (Num 25:10–13), the covenant of David (2 Sam 7:5–16), and the eternal covenant to be fulfilled through Christ, the new covenant (Jer 31:31–34; Luke 22:20). Following this pattern, I recommend that every pastor use a covenant ministry as a tool of accountability in the local body.

What follows is directly from the Covenant Ministry Manual we have developed for our local church body in Ashland. It begins with a cover letter that reads:

Dear Lay Leader,

We are people of covenant. God's people always have been, and always will be. Consider with me the precedent God has established in his Word: the covenant of Noah (Gen 9:8–17); the covenant of Abraham (Gen 15:9–21; 17); the covenant at Sinai (Ex 19–24); the covenant of Phinehas (Num 25:10–13); the covenant of David (2 Sam 7:5–16); and the new covenant (Jer 31:31–34; Heb 9:15). These are the major covenants that serve as our example of the binding relationship we have with God as his people, especially as leaders of his people. As the Church of God began to take form as a movement in the heart and mind of our pioneer, D. S. Warner, the example continued. Please consider the following insert from *Birth of a Reformation: The Life and Labors of Daniel S. Warner*. [See Appendix.]

In keeping with our biblical examples, that of our own D. S. Warner, and as a reflection of the qualifications for leadership found in Paul's letters to Timothy and Titus, attached you will find the Lay Leadership Covenant for the First Church of God. Please pray over this covenant and consider well your obligation to serve as a godly example to the congregation and the circle of influence around you. Then, knowing that the Word will guide you and the Spirit will empower you, sign the covenant and display it in a prominent place as a reminder of your willingness to serve in your capacity as a lay leader. Your pastoral staff has led the way, taking before the congregation their own covenants, and trusting in the same guidance and power as you for their fulfillment.

Thank you for your partnership in covenant ministry! Together, God will continue to use us to see the fulfillment of His Great Commission and Great Commandment. And keep our vision ever before you: "Jesus Christ: To Know Him, To Love Him, To Serve Him, and To Share Him!"

Serving with you,
Pastor Tom

Following are examples of our ministry covenants:

First Church of God & Wildwood Ministries: Lay Leadership Covenant

"For this we labor and strive." (1 Tim 4:10)

Understanding that I am called of God to serve His church, my eternal family, I attest that I have:

Been saved and baptized.

Prayed to be filled with the Spirit.

Further, that I will strive to:

Set an example in daily private prayer and Bible study.

Set an example in words of love and encouragement.

And to further dispel gossip in any form.

Set an example in attendance of corporate worship, discipleship, and important events in the life of the church.

Set an example in unity and harmony with the leadership, doctrines, and practices of the Church of God.

Set an example in tithing and joyful giving.

Set an example in exercising my gift with first fruits excellence.

I understand that I will be held in loving accountability for my example.

First Church of God & Wildwood Ministries: Elder's Covenant

"For this we labor and strive." (1 Tim 4:10)

Understanding that I am called of God to serve His church, my eternal family, I attest that I have:

Been saved and baptized.

Prayed to be filled with the Spirit.

Further, that I will strive to:

Set an example in daily private prayer and Bible study.

Set an example in words of love and encouragement.

And to further dispel gossip in any form.

Set an example in attendance of corporate worship, discipleship, and important events in the life of the church.

Set an example in unity and harmony with the leadership, doctrines, and practices of the Church of God.

Set an example in tithing and joyful giving.

Set an example in exercising my gift with first fruits excellence.

Further, I will also strive to:

Prayerfully seek, cast, and implement the visions God has given for ministry (Acts 2:17–18).

Faithfully guide and guard congregational unity and ministry momentum (John 17:20–23).

Fervently support and defend the pastoral staff and fellow lay leadership (1 Tim 17–22).

I understand that I will be held in loving accountability for my example.

First Church of God & Wildwood Ministries: Family Covenant
"For this we labor and strive." (1 Tim 4:10)

Knowing that being a part of the family is made possible through salvation in Jesus Christ alone, the first fruits of God the Father (1 Cor 15:20–23) I will commit to:

Give the first fruits of my thoughts (Ps 139:23; Phil 4:8).

Give the first fruits of my tongue (Ps 40:3; Eph 4:29–32).

Give the first fruits of my time (Hos 10:12; Matt 5:15–16).

Give the first fruits of my talents (Matt 25:14–30; 1 Cor 12:4–6).

Give the first fruits through my tithe (Mal 3:6–18; Luke 14:33).

I understand that the same Spirit that empowers me (Eph 3:14–21) to be faithful, and prunes me to be fruitful (John 15:1–8), will hold me accountable for my example (Heb 12:1–12) according to the blessed Word of God.

First Church of God & Wildwood Ministries: Senior Pastor

"For this we labor and strive." (1 Tim 4:10)

Understanding that I am called of God to serve His church, my eternal family, I attest that I have:

Been saved and baptized.

Prayed to be filled with the Spirit.

Accepted my divine call to the pastoral ministry.

Further, that I will strive to fulfill my role as:

Model of soul winning according to Matthew 28:18–20

Equipper of the saints for ministry according to Ephesians 4:11–12

Preacher and teacher of the gospel according to 2 Timothy 4:1–3

And to:

Set an example in words of love and encouragement.

Set an example in tithing and joyful giving.

Set an example in exercising my gift with first fruits excellence.

I understand that I will be held in loving accountability for my example.

First Church of God & Wildwood Ministries: Worship Arts Pastor

"For this we labor and strive." (1 Tim 4:10)

Understanding that I am called of God to serve His church, my eternal family, I attest that I have:

Been saved and baptized.

Prayed to be filled with the Spirit.

Accepted my divine call to the pastoral ministry.

Further, that I will strive to fulfill my role as:

Leader of musicians according to 1 Chronicles 25.

Designator of those selected to lead the people in praise according to 2 Chronicles 8:14.

Supervisor of the administrative team of the church according to 1 Corinthians 12:28.

And to:

Set an example in words of love and encouragement.

Set an example in tithing and joyful giving.

Set an example in exercising my gift with first fruits excellence.

First Church of God & Wildwood Ministries: Student Ministries Pastor

"For this we labor and strive." (1 Tim 4:10)

Understanding that I am called of God to serve His church, my eternal family, I attest that I have:

Been saved and baptized.

Prayed to be filled with the Spirit

Accepted my divine call to the pastoral ministry.

Further, that I will strive to:

Follow all vital elements of student ministry found in Ephesians 4:11–16.

Guided by the Holy Spirit, through prayer and total reliance.

Discipleship of young people in faith, knowledge, and practice.

Creating an environment of trust, based on truth and love.

Recognizing the value of each young person's life in God's eyes.

Creating opportunities for outreach and missions.

Seeking unity through quality relationships.

And to:

Set an example in words of love and encouragement.

Set an example in tithing and joyful giving.

Set an example in exercising my gift with first fruits excellence.

In God alone I trust!

For He alone is the author and perfector!

I understand that I will be held in loving accountability for my example.

First Church of God & Wildwood Ministries: Children's Ministry Pastor

"For this we labor and strive." (1 Tim 4:10)

Understanding that I am called of God to serve His church, my eternal family, I attest that I have:

Been saved and baptized.

Prayed to be filled with the Spirit.

Accepted my divine call to the pastoral ministry.

Further, that I will:

Equip God's people to minister to children.

Faithfully tell children the glorious deeds of God and the gospel of Jesus Christ.

Come alongside and support parents as they train up their children.

Receive children in Christ's name seeking to remove any obstacles in their lives.

And to:

Set an example in words of love and encouragement.

Set an example in tithing and joyful giving.

Set an example in exercising my gift with first fruits excellence.

Covenant Ministry: Implementation and Outcome

"Let your gentleness be evident to all. The Lord is near" (Phil 4:5). Although this passage does not speak of covenants in particular, it does speak directly to our day-to-day living as children of God and is especially applicable to our methodology of church leadership. Covenant ministry is not ruling with an iron fist. Rather, it is leading with sure and gentle strength. Another analogy is to consider covenant ministry as one of the vital building blocks of your ministry, "velvet-covered bricks" you will use to lay and establish firm foundations.[3]

---

3. Howard E. Butt, *The Velvet Covered Brick* (New York: Harper and Row, 1973).

Implementation

Consider the following as a guide to implementing a covenant ministry.

1. *Candidacy.* When entering into a time of candidacy for pastoral ministry, set forth as part of your ministry the clear intention to implement covenant ministry. Prepare a handout such as this explaining covenant ministry. Prepare an example of your own covenant and be prepared to discuss the process in detail with your potential partners in ministry. You are making a statement: This is who I am and how I envision we will operate in leadership throughout our ministry.

2. *Preaching and Teaching.* Share with your congregation a series of sermons or small-group studies concerning covenants as well as accountability in relationships (between individuals, the church, and God). Emphasize the biblical precedent and that of our own Church of God heritage concerning covenant relationships, especially covenant leadership.

3. *Ministry Planning.* Schedule a time of planning with your leadership. Give them a sense of ownership in this concept and develop it together. Prepare a rough draft of your covenant ministry plan, then gather input from your leadership concerning the preparation and final wording of your covenants. This vision must be shared and supported by your leadership. It almost goes without stating that the standard put forth will be tested. Thus, you must have a united front with your ministry leaders when the time comes to use the covenants as a tool of accountability.

4. *Modeling.* At an appropriate time, take your covenant before the congregation. Do this before or at the same time as your lay leadership commits to theirs. Then keep the covenant statement with you and display it prominently in your office. Refer to it often as one of God's tools for your own spiritual growth and accountability. Of

course, require the same of all additional ministry staff who come on board in the future.

5. *Applying Covenant Commitments.* Again, the covenant standard for leadership will be tested. Consider the following as a possible procedure for using covenants with your leadership when the time comes to hold someone accountable. Keep Matthew 18 handy as the guide throughout.

First, do not hold someone accountable alone. Call for a time of sharing with the individual and take a trusted lay leader with you who will serve to keep you accountable to a gentle, loving spirit, and who will also serve as a witness to the time of sharing for all parties involved.

Second, assume there is a spiritual need first and not a lack of accountability to any part of the covenant. Ask the leader in question what need they may have and what you can pray about before you confront the area that needs to be addressed.

Third, give them the opportunity to share and explain why they have not kept their commitment. Hasty accusations on your part will serve no purpose but to potentially weaken your leadership position and future influence.

Fourth, refer all parties present to the covenant that the leader has signed. Read the sections that may be applicable to the individual. Assure them that your goal is to meet any spiritual needs they may have and to help them set an example in the future that all leaders has agreed is the biblical standard for leadership. Stress the need for all church leaders to be united in setting this example. Be gentle in affirming that further, willful compromises in these areas are unacceptable and will call into question the leader's suitability for leadership. Perhaps you could suggest a time of prayer and careful personal reflection before the leader makes a recommitment to the covenant example. (Use your Spirit-led judgment on each of these points.) End the session with a season of prayer for further strength and guidance as you seek to continue in covenant leadership.

Outcome

What will covenants do for your local ministry? Covenants provide opportunities for you to train your people, especially your pastoral and lay leaders in the areas of accountability, doctrine, and personal example. Take time to refer to the various areas of emphasis in your covenant and study them from the Word together.

Covenants set forth the biblical standards for leadership that are often unwritten in any form (except perhaps in an antiquated set of bylaws that have long since been filed away). Unfortunately, these standards also go unspoken in most congregations. Thus, the congregation has only a vague standard for leadership that is loosely followed. The only recourse when there is a need for accountability is to fall back on generalities such as, "We do things the Bible way!" or "You ought to know better." Covenants describe the Bible way more specifically concerning leadership in local church ministry.

Covenants provide an objective tool for accountability. Issues are elevated above the personal and can be addressed from the context of a higher, unified standard for all. No one, especially the pastor, is picking on anyone. Rather, everyone is held to the same standard and desires to prayerfully encourage others in reflecting that standard as church leaders.

Covenants help reestablish a sense of pastoral authority and influence. This sense has been unquestionably eroded in the last quarter century due to highly publicized moral and ethical failures of some prominent spiritual leaders. Covenants lend an authority and influence based on the standard of the Word, not on the pastor's length of tenure, age, or popularity with an influential group in the church (who may or may not actually be in formal leadership). Further, the pastor can hold forth the covenant standard, knowing that nothing is being asked of lay leaders that is not first required of the pastor. The precedent is set, the example is modeled, and authority and influence are accepted, based on the authority of the Word and not a set of vague subjective standards.

Covenant ministry will not end disagreement or disunity in the local church. However, this biblical model for leadership will certainly lessen opportunities for the Enemy to sow seeds of bitterness and discord. Much prayer should accompany this or any other endeavor, giving full sway to the Holy Spirit as the Word of God is held forth as the final authority. Covenants may be the most appropriate tools to gently build a new ministry from the ground up or help reestablish an existing ministry's leadership team on a firmer biblical foundation.

12.

Unbelief

And he did not many miracles there because of their lack of faith.
—*Matthew 13:58*

"**L**ORD, as I preach, help me to communicate clearly, and help them to get it, to understand!" Countless times over the years, every time that I have been blessed to preach the gospel, I have prayed variations of this. And by his grace, the Lord has answered. However, recently I have been challenged to realize that, in fact, I am praying for only half of what I should. I have since been spending less and less time praying for knowledge and more and more time praying for faith.

I came to this realization as I prepared for a series of sermons on divine healing and deliverance. After more than a month of study, I realized that I didn't totally get it and none of the many theologians I had studied got it, either. I further realized that I wasn't likely to fully understand these truths, period—at least not on this side of heaven. However, that didn't seem to matter. At some point, the great preachers of the church have set their reasoning aside and just believed. So I have come to the place where belief is at least as important to my ministry as knowledge, perhaps even more so.

We have come to believe only in a very limited sense that God is moving in and through us, his people. We can muster enough faith to believe God will send an occasional decision for salvation, a rare restoration of someone who has fallen away, an extraordinary healing, or a sudden growth in attendance. We comfort ourselves by rationalizing. "After all, these are the last days. No one is hungry for the truth any more. We can't expect to do much better than this." And so we go on celebrating our survival. Sadly, this has become the norm.

What is the solution? I believe it's time for the church to get back to normal, to truly believe God for miracles once again. What can this possibly mean? By getting back to normal, I don't mean the nominal religiosity we have resigned ourselves to. I mean New Testament normal. And just what is this? It is a situation where we frequently see decisions for Christ, divine healings, spiritual restorations, deliverance from evil spirits, hunger for the Word of God, and crowds. Yes, New Testament normal is a situation in which large crowds are constantly gathering because something out of the ordinary is happening. Isn't this one of the distinguishing features of our character as the children of God? Not a few times we are referred to as a "peculiar" people (Ex 19:5; Deut 14:2; 26:18; Ps 135:4; Tit 2:14; 1 Pet 2:9). The outflow of our peculiar character will be uncommon manifestations of the practically miraculous! Can we not dare to begin believing in the New Testament normal once again? What are we waiting for? What is holding us back? Is it perhaps fear?

We fear failure. What if we start claiming the New Testament norm and God doesn't show up as we advertise? What if we prepare and promote for two hundred more people to attend our annual turkey dinner and fail to even match last year's attendance? What if we claim the promise of divine healing and only end up disappointing the sufferer, or worse, being party to the disillusionment of someone who was only seeking a touch from the Lord? Well, most of us are in no danger of finding out!

What kind of faithless reasoning are we using, anyway? Is God's Word not still in effect? Take a moment to read John 12:9–14; Acts 2:17–21; 1 Corinthians 2:9–10; and Ephesians 3:20–21. How can we settle for anything less than what has been foretold and promised to us by the precious Word of God? If his Word is as valid today as it was in the first century for doctrinal teaching, then it must be equally valid today for its promise of miraculous manifestations of his Spirit. Or have we resigned this to the charismatics?

It's really a matter of humility. We must be humble enough to stop worrying about being humiliated, seen as failures, misunderstood, and misrepresented in the eyes of either saint or sinner.

We fear success almost as much as we fear failure. If we dare to believe and audaciously act on the belief for more of the miraculous acts of God and then God shows himself in those miraculous ways, we will have some explaining to do. We will have some changes to make. Our daily witness will change (Acts 4:18–22). Our comfort zone will be compromised. Our lives will be cramped and crowded with more and more people drawn by an uncommon move of God.

Oh, Church of God, we must believe God for more! We have every reason to believe the precious promises of God and act upon them. Pastor Jim Cymbala shares a challenging thought as he reflects on Joshua 1:2–5. He writes,

> Christians will never know what God can do through them until they step out and dare to attempt what he's called them to do. It is always in the place where we dare to "set our foot" that God manifests his power. There can be no real anointing of the Spirit while we sit on the sidelines. The blessing and the help of God were promised to Israel as they took action. Like us, the Israelites would have liked it the other way around, "Lord, as we're praying here, please bring the land to us!" But the Lord was saying, "No, cross a river that's not crossable and face enemies stronger than you. Get up and possess what I promised! I'll only give you where you walk. If you won't dare to go there, I won't give it to you."[1]

We have got to believe. We must get beyond ourselves and all of the norms we have adjusted to and believe God for the extraordinary.

---

1. Jim Cymbala, "Going to the Next Level," *The Messenger Newsletter* 1, no. 5 (November 2004).

13.

The Church Growth Movement

All over the world this gospel is bearing fruit and growing, just as it has been doing among you since the day you heard it and understood God's grace in all its truth. —Colossians 1:6

THE DEBATE has been going on far too long and will likely continue. The question: Is modern church growth a sign of the movement of the Holy Spirit or merely the predicted assembly of a faithless people with "itching ears" (2 Tim 4:3)? Let's hear both sides of the argument.

On one hand are those who believe that exponential church growth cannot possibly be a move of the Holy Spirit. After all, they remember that Jesus said, "Small is the gate and narrow the road that leads to life and only a few find it" (Matt 7:14). He also said, "The laborers are few" (Matt. 9:37). People who hold this view believe that the masses are being deceived by liberal false prophets who cannot possibly be preaching the truth or else they would not be drawing such crowds. They condemn easy belief-ism, watered-down gospel, cheap grace, and entertainment, instead of worship, seeker-friendly ministry, marketing the gospel, and so on. They exclaim, "Many will be deceived in the last days—and that's just what this is! The tried-and-true traditional methods of ministry work just fine for those who are truly seeking God." They hold fast to a belief that masses of people won't be attracted to a truly sanctified way of life. Only a few will hear and believe the truth. "But that's all right," they say, "because numbers don't matter."

On the other hand are those who believe in a great gathering of God's people in the last days, a spiritual harvest like never before. "The harvest is plentiful," they remind us (Matt 9:37). They focus on God's promise that "I will pour out my Spirit on all people…and everyone who calls on the name of the Lord will be saved" (Acts 2:17, 21). They respond to their critics by saying, "The masses are just the ones who need to hear the gospel! Jesus was seeker friendly. Salvation is worth celebrating! Don't be so heavenly-minded that you are no earthly good. Further, God is doing a new thing! We have got to be willing to change, to meet people where they live." These Christians hold fast to their belief that the more Jesus is lifted up, the more people will be drawn to him. They say, "We count people because people count to Christ."

To be quite honest, I have sat on both sides of the aisle at different stages in my leadership journey. I have sought to resolve the debate in my own mind and find a solution in my own life and local ministry. There is truth to be found in both mindsets, and I pray that I continue to learn from them. However, I cannot straddle the fence on this issue. None of us in ministry have the luxury of sitting on the sidelines for very long. After taking a brief look at the book of Acts for insight into this conflict, we may want to address a deeper, more pertinent question: what is my motive for the side I have taken?

What does the book of Acts tell us about church growth? Quite a bit:

> 1:15—The church started with "a group numbering about a hundred and twenty."

> 1:26—"Matthias…was added to the eleven apostles."

> 2:5—People "came from every nation."

> 2:6—"A crowd came together…"

> 2:21—"And everyone" responded to the message.

> 2:39—It was for "you and your children and for all who are far off."

2:41—"About three thousand were added to their number that day."

2:47d—"And the Lord added daily those who were being saved."

3:9–10—"When all of the people saw...they were filled with wonder and amazement."

4:4—"But many who heard the message believed [and the church] grew to about five thousand."

5:14—"More and more men and women believed in the Lord and were added to their number."

5:16—"Crowds gathered."

6:1—"In those days when the number of disciples was increasing."

6:7—"So the word of God spread...[the] number of disciples increased rapidly...[to] a large number."

8:3—They preached from "house to house" (my favorite evidence of an apostolic small-group ministry!).

8:6—"The crowds heard."

8:7—"Evil spirits came out of many."

8:12—Both men and women were baptized in Samaria.

8:25—The apostles were "preaching the gospel in many Samaritan villages."

8:29—"The Spirit told Phillip, 'Go' (My favorite command!).

8:30—"Then Phillip ran."

9:31—"The church throughout Judea, Galilee, and Samaria... [was] strengthened, encouraged, ...grew in numbers."

9:35—"All those who lived in Lydda and Sharon saw him and turned to the Lord."

9:42—The gospel "became known all over Joppa, and many believed."

10:27—"Peter...found a large gathering of people."

10:35—"But [God] accepts men from every nation."

10:37—"You know what has happened throughout Judea."

11:18—"God has granted even the Gentiles repentance."

11:20—The apostles "began to speak to Greeks also."

11:21—"And a great number of people believed and turned."

11:24—"And a great number of people were brought to the Lord."

11:26—They "taught great numbers of people."

12:24—"The word of God continued to increase and spread."

13:43—"Many of the Jews and devout converts to Judaism followed" the evangelists.

13:44—"Almost the whole city gathered to hear the word of the Lord."

13:49—"The Word of the Lord spread throughout the whole region."

14:1—"There they spoke so effectively that a great number of Jews and Gentiles believed."

14:21—"And won a large number of disciples."

15:35—"And many others taught and preached the word of the Lord."

16:5—"So the churches were strengthened in the faith and grew daily in numbers."

16:15—Lydia and her household were baptized.

16:33—The Philippian jailer and his household were baptized.

17:4—Some Jews believed the gospel, "as did a large number of God-fearing Greeks and not a few prominent women."

17:12—"Many of the Jews believed, as did also a number of prominent Greek women and many Greek men."

17:13—Paul brought agitation and a stirring to the "crowds."

17:34—"A few men became followers...[as well as] a woman named Damaris, and a number of others."

18:8—"Crispus...and his entire household...many of the Corinthians...believed and were baptized."

19:10—"All the Jews and Greeks who lived in the province of Asia heard the Word of the Lord."

19:11—"God did extraordinary miracles through Paul."

19:20—The "word of the Lord spread widely and grew in power."

19:26—"Large numbers" were convinced by Paul.

20:20—The apostles "taught you publicly and from house to house."

21:20—"You see, brother, how many thousands of Jews have believed."

21:30—"The whole city was aroused, and the people came running from all directions" to hear what they were saying.

21-28—Paul's arrest and trials.

28:30—"Boldly and without hindrance [Paul] preached the kingdom of God and taught about the Lord Jesus Christ."

What are your observations? Please don't take mine as a complete analysis, but my observations have led me to the following conclusions:

As a direct result of the infilling of the Holy Spirit, the purity of the message proclaimed, and the willingness of God's people to be moved by the Spirit, the early church was characterized by exponential growth! In the book of Acts, numbers *do* seem to matter and were, in fact, recorded. However, numbers themselves were never the stated objective. Crowds and the masses are considered to be good things when gathered in order to hear the gospel.

Rather than having a sense of exclusiveness or feeling that they were a holy huddle, the early Christians had a sense of inclusiveness that permeated their entire ministry. They had no paralyzing fear of doctrinal contamination. Didn't Peter, Stephen, Paul, Barnabas, and Silas preach the gospel, setting forth the example of holy living as they went? At the same time, were they not willing to lay aside their own traditions and do whatever was necessary to reach people at the point, place, and time of their need with the life-changing message of Jesus Christ? The message of the early church was holy contemporary.

The church of the book of Acts is our best model for ministry. Its power is our power; its teachings our teachings; its challenges our challenges; its numbers our numbers; its victory ours! No doubt some will yet maintain that church growth was only a first-century thing. I would ask, What about Jesus' example? Were his miracles and influence exclusively his? Or did he really mean it when he said, "I tell you the truth, anyone who has faith in me will do what I have been doing. He will do even greater things than these, because I am going to the Father"? (John 14:12). And what of God's indication of his power in and through his people as recorded in Ephesians 3:20–21? "Now to him who is able to do immeasurably more than all we ask or imagine, according to his power that is at work within us, to him be glory in the church and in Christ Jesus throughout all generations, for ever and ever! Amen."

Perhaps I am a bit naïve to believe in a great harvest in the midst of a "crooked and depraved generation" (Phil 2:15). However, I believe that, not only is there a quickening of the souls of seekers, but there is also a gathering of believers for this very purpose, and it's called the Church of God!

> Rejoice, be glad! The Shepherd has begun,
> His long divided flock again to gather into one.[1]

Let us return to the question of motive. If my motive as a pastor is to see my congregation become big numerically as evidence of divine favor and blessing, then my theology is uninformed and wanting. If my motive is to prove my critics wrong, then my priority is misplaced. If my motive is to prove the effectiveness of a certain methodology or style of ministry, then I am limiting God's power and just plain missing

---

1. Charles W. Naylor, "The Church's Jubilee," in *Worship the Lord: Hymnal of the Church of God* (Anderson, IN: Warner Press, 1989), 312.

his point in all of this. Church growth is not about me, my methodology, or my ministry style, but about Jesus Christ—crucified, risen, and coming again! And lost people are waiting for us to bring this message to them.

There are several sources of numerical church growth, each of which is ordained of God, in my opinion. There is transfer growth. This results from the Spirit leading one beggar to tell another beggar where to find bread. This kind of growth (at least in our ministry) is not the result of sheep stealing, the active pursuit of individuals and families presently attending other fellowships. People may begin attending our congregation simply because they now see the church as they have never seen it before. Perhaps they simply want to be in a place where their spiritual needs, and those of their children, are met. Perhaps they desire to belong to a group of people who are full of divine passion, promise, and purpose. Isn't this what many people are looking for— only to find that it has a name, the Church of God?

There is seeker growth. Some well-meaning individuals are scornful of this type of growth because they simply are afraid of non-Christians living and breathing in their midst. Many of our people have grown accustomed to seeing the same faces of the faithful week after week, month after month, and year after year. I would suggest to you that there are not enough sinners attending our local-church ministries, our small groups, or our corporate worship services. No, I do not believe there is such a thing as seeker worship, because worship must be in "spirit and in truth" (John 4:24). Seekers can indeed sing, maybe even learn some of our moves, and be deeply touched, motivated, amused, even stirred, convicted, and drawn; but they will truly worship only when they are saved and the Holy Spirit fills them, making true worship of the Father possible. However, the Father loves a full house and he commands us to make room for more (Luke 14:21–24). He expects us to provide more ways for the lost to "taste and see" that he is good (Ps 34:8) and claim their place at his table, set for them at the greatest cost, the blood of Jesus Christ. The broad criticism of seeker-friendly ministries, based on a few extreme examples, is little more than legalism. It is only a backhand swipe at unfamiliar and nontraditional methodologies that may help to open the door of the Kingdom to the lost (Matt 23:13–14).

The best form of growth is salvation growth! On this there is no debate. However, weren't new converts seekers before they were saved? They were lost and they were seeking, even if they did not know what (let alone who) they were seeking. Then they were found by God. Whether they confessed Christ in line at Wal-Mart, at a small-group meeting, at the office, at a Saturday night worship service, or at school, they were lost and now they are found in Jesus Christ.

I pray that the criticism of church growth will cease because the ungodly sense of fear has been removed. It's a fear of spiritual success—in short, a fear of seekers coming because saints are going. I envision a church where people are being saved and sanctified, where their hands are being set to the plow in God's vineyard, and where no one is looking back, because together we are becoming less and less like our preconceived notions of the church and more and more like the one in the book of Acts that serves as our model.

14.

Prophets' Profits

The elders who direct the affairs of the church well are worthy of double honor, especially those whose work is preaching and teaching. —1 Timothy 5:17

ADEQUATE pastoral provision is clearly conveyed throughout Scripture by principle, command, and example. In short, the Word of God reveals that when the people honor their prophets, God honors the people. This cannot be emphasized enough throughout our movement. I try to touch on it at every opportunity on behalf of my fellow servants. I can say for them what they may not feel comfortable saying to their lay leadership or what the lay leadership has trouble telling the congregation. (Please do the same for your fellow ministers at every turn!) Unfortunately, the biblical concept of double honor is opposed by an unspoken tradition in the Church of God: keep him poor, keep him humble. That miserly tradition has quenched the Spirit of God and played no small role in keeping local church bodies from reaching their full potential in ministry.

Granted, there is always great temptation to be greedy for money, and God's servants are not immune to it (Jer 6:13–15). However, the few who have merited the accusation of being in it for the money do not represent the vast majority of pastors, who understand that the ministry is certainly no get-rich-quick scheme. The overwhelming majority of ministers have answered a call that will take them far from home and require sacrifices that God does not ask of most of the spiritual family.

The people of Ashland First Church of God have served as an exemplary model of provision in the past and seek to continue to do so in the future. Consider the following texts and brief commentary that we have included in a document on ministers' compensation:

Deuteronomy 15:7–11. This speaks to the general principle and spirit of giving. It should be noted that if this applies to any brother or sister, then it applies equally to the pastor, who first became a brother or sister, then a pastor.

Deuteronomy 25:4; 1 Corinthians 9:1–12; 1; Timothy 5:17–18. These passages speak directly to the subject of pastoral provision. "Muzzling the ox" is an illustration that speaks of the pastoral leadership's ability to work for the church with continued strength by having adequate provision, unencumbered by undue secular worries and cares. The stronger and healthier the oxen, the more they can pull, haul, and till. This must be of great significance, because the Word of God gives this command three different times (Deut 25:4; 1 Cor 9:9; 1 Tim 5:18), spanning both the old and new covenants. Further, the pastoral leadership should receive provision in greater proportion with respect to others in the ministry. "All the more" is the guiding spirit clearly indicated by the apostle Paul. Finally, honor is always a good thing to bestow on anyone and at any time, and much of Scripture refers to honoring those who deserve it. However, only in reference to pastoral leadership does Scripture set the standard of "double honor."

1 Chronicles 16:22; Psalms 105:15; Ecclesiastes 11:1; Luke 6:38. Consider well that God has his watchful eye on those whom he has called into the ministry. Numerous examples in both the Old and New Testament speak of God's vengeful protection of his prophets, shepherds, and disciples (see passages above, also Josh 23:9–11). But God uses positive reinforcement as well. To ensure the kind of provision he feels his prophets deserve, he promises the same reward for those who honor them as he does for the prophets themselves!

These passages also reveal that receiving is proportional to giving. In one passage, the measure of receiving is at least equal to the giving; in another, far more is received than was originally invested. As the Spirit of the Lord blesses a ministry, there is most often a direct correlation between the prosperity and effectiveness of that ministry and the investment made in and by the pastoral staff. A congregation is blessed by God as the pastors are provided for and they, in turn, are encouraged to give their all in the ministry. Of course, most pastors set a high personal standard in tithes and offerings and give a large portion of their compensation right back into the church and ministry—in tangible ways, as well as those known only by the Father.

Also note that pastors are a direct reflection on the spiritual health of the local church body. A godly pride in the ministry will be reflected by a people who consider their pastoral staff the chief "ambassadors" of the Lord and the church (2 Cor 5:20). The pastoral staff will be representing the congregation both in professional and ministry settings, and should be in a position to do so honorably.

Deuteronomy 23:20; Psalm 37:26; Psalm 112:5; Proverbs 11:25. These passages speak of the lending process. When a gift cannot be extended, a loan is considered a godly way of providing for members of God's family, and that without interest. Further, this type of lending implies trust for repayment without undue secular means of guarantee. In truth, if a brother or sister (let alone a member of the pastoral staff) cannot be trusted to repay a loan, then they should not be entrusted with leadership. This trust is also extended by pastors, who do not lord over their knowledge of the people's giving record concerning tithes and offerings.

Luke 10:2–7. This passage describes the context of pastoral ministry. Each disciple is a lamb among wolves. The pastoral ministry is tough business—in fact, tougher than most. The lack of clergy nationwide reflects this fact as fewer and fewer answer the call, while many others are leaving pastoral ministry at alarming rates. The Enemy knows that if he can strike the shepherd, the sheep will scatter (Zech. 13:7). He uses this tactic by disproportionately concentrating attacks on pastors and lay leaders in their day-to-day lives. Inherent to the position of minister is the lack of familial support that a larger portion of the laity enjoys and often takes for granted (Luke 14:25–27). Pastors seldom live near their parents, siblings, or extended family and cannot rely on them for material aid. This is part of the price that is paid. The local church body cannot take the place of a pastor's family; however, the church can acknowledge this in other forms of loving support by providing fellowship and the financial resources to conduct the ministry.

Finally, the Luke 10 passage makes it clear that shepherds should travel light. However, this does not contradict the rest of the counsel of the Word of God, nor does it justify meager provisions for pastors or our state and national leaders. Rather, it assumes that God will provide for their needs through the generous giving of those to whom they minister. The bottom line is that pastors and state or national church leaders provide for their own families and have the same obligations as any other spouse or parent (1 Tim 5:7–8). Longevity of ministry is also linked to ample provision for the leader, who should have no reason or incentive to move around from house to house in order to make ends meet. Consider the much higher rate of long-term pastorates in the National Association of the Church of God. Might this correlate with African Americans' white glove treatment of their pastors, compared to that of predominantly white congregations? I spoke about this with Pastor Timothy Clarke, former presiding elder of the National Association. He confirmed that a much higher level of respect and honor of the clergy is typical in the National Association. He also assured me that generous financial compensation, though not to ungodly excess, is part of this honor.

This is a brief look at the biblical principles of provision for pastoral leaders in the local body. Although distinctly called of God, pastors and their families are real people with real hopes, real hurts, real dreams, and needs. They understand and accept the sacrifices of their calling. The general lack of provision in many Church of God congregations is partly due to a false interpretation of Scripture and not the congregation's lack of genuine love and respect for their pastors and leaders. Let us confess that it is also partly due to our unwillingness as leaders to tell our people about our financial burdens and frustrations, even though we have known in our spirits that something has never been quite right.

May our local congregations and our movement as a whole seek to give double honor to our leaders as never before. In the final analysis, God is being honored and he will be given all the glory as he prospers his church.

15.

First Fruits

But seek first the kingdom of God and His righteousness, and all these things will be given to you as well. —Matthew 6:33

OUR CAPACITY to bear spiritual fruit is in direct proportion to the extent to which we employ the scriptural principle of first fruits in our ministry life and witness. The reason for this is simple: God demands and deserves our first fruits, and he blesses accordingly.

What do we mean by the principle of first fruits? It is the concept of giving God the best we possess. Whether it is the best of our time, our talents, our material resources, even our emotions, we are to give God the first choice of what we have. This philosophy of life and ministry finds its roots in the story of Cain and Abel.

Genesis 4 tells us that both Cain and Abel brought an offering to the Lord. Cain's offering was described as being "some of the fruits" (v. 3), while Abel brought "fat portions from some of the firstborn of his flock" (v. 4). Cain knew that his offering (which would have been an altogether generous and acceptable gift to anyone else) was not an acceptable offering to the One who created the very soil he tilled and gained his livelihood from. However, instead of confessing, repenting, and making restitution to God with a true first fruits offering, Cain took out his guilt on his brother. As a result, Cain was cursed for life (vv. 11–12). I would suggest that we, too, are under a curse in direct proportion to our unwillingness to give God what he demands and deserves, the first fruits of our lives.

"We are supposed to be good stewards," some will say. "Surely we can find something cheaper."

"What about our savings account? What if we don't have enough for an emergency?"

"I don't think we should get that for our church. No other church in our area seems to need one."

"That looks okay, just fine. After all, it's a church, not a show room."

"We can just take care of that real quick when we get there. That's what we did last year and nobody said anything about it."

"I know someone else can do a better job and are more gifted for that work, but we don't want to hurt anyone's feelings or cause a problem. Brother and Sister Jones have done it for years. They would throw a fit if we asked someone else!"

"We've gotten along just fine without that until now. We must not need it."

On and on go the rationalizations for having a ministry based on second fruits and gifts that will do. How dare we do this in the name of the Lord in full view of a world that sees him through us, the very body of Christ?

If I were to rate the overall quality of service at the Church of God congregations where I have been blessed to minister over the years, I would give us a "good" rating—a solid B. However, seeing that the scale of ministry service probably includes A and even A+, this rating simply is not good enough. Most of us can do better and we know it. After all, we find ways to do better in most other areas of our lives. Deep down, we know this to be true.

I'm not suggesting that we insist on doing Christian ministry in a *Lifestyles of the Rich and Famous* kind of way. Perhaps the best we can do isn't the best on the market, but it should be *our* best. And if we can take a leap of faith to give the very best the market has to offer, then we should give no less.

I recently saw a great example of first-fruits philosophy when I received a formal invitation in the mail. The return address was in Atlanta, Georgia. I quickly thought of a few people I knew there. *Who is getting married?* I wondered. *Is someone retiring?* The invitation was beautiful. The envelope was thick and textured, obviously not a bulk-rate stock. My name and address were written in a formal script; its form spoke of elegance and grace. As I opened the envelope and pulled out the bifold card, a fragile piece of translucent rice paper floated out gracefully on currents of unseen air—a subtle extra that added just the right touch of class. Then I read the invitation. To my surprise, I discovered that I did not know the happy couple and I am quite sure they don't know me, not personally. You see, this was an announcement to all "valued customers" of AT&T and Cingular Wireless formalizing their recent merger.

I thought, *Wow! How many of these did they send out? Why not save money and send a postcard like...like this one?* I compared the corporate announcement to a card from a local Christian organization that I had received that same day. It was a single, thin, plain, bulk-rate card with a jumble of various sizes and styles of type. Apparently, the senders had tried to scrunch in as much information as possible on the one card. My innate response was immediate: one group wanted my attention and valued my interest more than the other.

Regardless of our protests that our hearts are in the right place, ministry is really about making statements of value. In how we present ourselves, in how far we will go to meet a need, make someone comfortable, or make a positive first impression—yes, in how we care for our facilities and how we conduct ministry—we make statements of value. We are not placing value on appearances, things, or status; we are placing value on other beings, both human and divine.

> Jesus emphasized the importance of prioritizing others, second only to loving God with all our strength (see Mark 12:33). The way we love others is by serving them and meeting their needs. If we believe the Bible teaches that we must serve others out of reverence for Christ, and that people are going to spend an eternity in hell without our winning them for the Kingdom, then we must continually improve our methodologies to save some. The Church is a service-oriented organization.[1]

---

1. Stan Toler and Alan Nelson, *The Five Star Church* (Ventura, CA: Regal Books, 1999), 23.

"You mean I should give my first fruits in everything I do for God?" you may exclaim. Yes, in everything, you should give God nothing but wholehearted excellence (see Col 3:17, 23). However, do not try to begin doing it in everything all at once! This is crucial to implementing a ministry of first fruits; you can't expect to do it all in a day. You will have to exercise the power of prayerful discernment as to which relationships and in which ministries to begin applying this principle. John Maxwell explains this concept of ministry priorities in his book *Today Matters*:

> Author Robert J. McKain says, "The reason most goals are not achieved is that we spend our time doing second things first." Let's face it; there are a lot of things vying for your attention. Many people want to put you on their agenda. Thousands of manufacturers want you to spend your money on their products. Even your own desires can be so diverse and your attention so scattered that you often aren't sure what should get your concentration. That's why you need to focus. To be successful, you can't just run on the fast track. People who reach their potential and fulfill their dreams determine and act on their priorities daily.[2]

I have discovered this to be true time and again. A case in point is our outdated church sanctuary at Ashland. Now, many would consider this to be a priority. It is, in fact, a tangible expression of God's character and presence, so it is very important. However, in our case, it isn't the most important thing—at least not yet. I recall the pulpit committee chairman and his wife apologizing for the worn and outdated condition of the church facilities as they gave us the nickel tour. They assured me that the church's leaders had every intention of getting right on it. I gave them the best compliment I could as I quickly angled my response in a positive direction. "No, these spaces are great," I said. "So much could be done here!" However, more than three years later, most of our facilities still have that groovy kind of late-'70s paneled thing going on!

---

2. John Maxwell, *Today Matters* (New York: Warner Faith, 2004): 68–69.

"How is that giving God your first fruits?" you might ask. Although we are now in the process of making those renovations (and can already envision the glory they will give God), we determined that our first priority at Ashland would be to acquire and develop the best pastoral and lay leadership, enlist their ministry teams, and equip them all with the latest and greatest training and supplies. Guess what? We have grown and grown and grown as people looked right past the dated skin of our ministry into our hearts of first-fruits excellence, proved by our investments.

This principle of first-fruits ministry must be motivated by our Lord and Savior, Jesus Christ. You see, God gave us his first fruits in him! "But Christ has indeed been raised from the dead, the firstfruits of those who have fallen asleep…Christ, the firstfruits…" (1 Cor 15:20, 23). To us—who were so unworthy, deserving of God's wrath and condemnation—he gave the best the whole universe had to offer.

Worthy, worthy, worthy is the One who has given his best for us! Let us offer to him, through him, and for him in the presence of all people nothing but our very best—our first fruits.

16.

Let the Fire Fall on Me!

John answered them all, "I baptize you with water. But one more powerful than I will come, the thongs of whose sandals I am not worthy to untie. He will baptize you with the Holy Spirit and with fire." —Luke 3:16

AFTER deliberating, discussing, and debating; after visioning, voting, and venting; after instigating, investigating, and implementing until we are dizzy concerning the problems and solutions facing us as a movement, it still comes down this: We need the fire of the Lord. Or, as I heard the Reverend David Hall, Chairperson of the Church of God Ministries Council, shout, "We must put the *move* back in the movement!"

Let me ask you, in the story of Elijah and the prophets of Baal (1 Kings 18), which role would we want to play as a movement? Do we want to be Elijah? Do we want to be the prophets of Baal? (Certainly not!) Perhaps we want to be the excited onlookers, who just came to see the show? Before you answer, consider whether there might be another option. Ask yourself if there isn't another role for the Church of God movement to play.

Could it be that we have failed to understand who (or what) God placed at the center of this event? It's the sacrifice—not any of the human players at all, but the sacrifice! "Then the fire of the Lord fell and burned up the sacrifice, the wood, the stones, and the soil, and also licked up the water in the trench" (1 Kings 18:38).

Why do servant-leaders want to play Elijah's part and not even begin to think about being the sacrifice? Because Elijah triumphs and remains the undisputed champion of the prophets in his day. We want to be champions too! Besides, everyone loves a winner.

But Elijah's victory was won in and through the sacrifice. Without the sacrifice there would be no victory. Come to think of it, every spiritual victory has been won through sacrifice. Our Lord and Savior Jesus Christ did not merely make a sacrifice—he *was* the sacrifice! As his ministers, we should be no less. "Therefore, I urge you, brothers, in view of God's mercy, to offer your bodies as living sacrifices, holy and pleasing to God—this is your spiritual act of worship" (Rom 12:1).

Note that Elijah's offering (a bull) was indeed sacrificial, but the methodology was sacrificial as well. Elijah went through the trouble of taking twelve stones, "one for each of the tribes," and built an altar. He dug a trench around that altar that could hold more than enough water to prove God's point. He carefully arranged the wood, cut the bull into pieces, and laid the sacrifice on the wood. He had four large jars filled with water and poured onto the wood, then did it again, then again! Elijah prayed heaven down and stepped back in faith to receive God's reply. It was fire. The "fire of the Lord" came in response to his faith and sacrificial efforts. That fire not only burnt the sacrifice, it burned the wood and the stones and the very soil, licking up the water without a trace! Oh, that we were that kind of sacrifice! If only we were ready and willing to be used—indeed, used up completely—for God's glory! Be the sacrifice, Church of God. Be the sacrifice!

We should say a word about one quencher of the Spirit of God, worldliness. It is entirely possible to be in the world and not of it, to be relevant and accessible to the world without being contaminated by it. But we must not embrace the ways of the world or allow our people to do the same. A. W. Tozer speaks well concerning the problem of worldliness among the people of God:

> Let the Bible experts split it up however they will, let them divide and subdivide it, then tack on a couple of Greek verbs. But when they are through, I will still believe that the kingdom of God is the realm of the Holy Spirit into which men and women enter when they are born from above. Yes, that invisible world that God has revealed is more real, more lasting, more eternal that this world we are in now. That is

why God has given us the prophets and His revelation in His Word. He wants us to be able to look in on the coming world…Of all the calamities that have been visited upon this world and its inhabitants, the willing surrender of the human spirit to materialistic values is the worst! We who were made for higher worlds are accepting the ways of this world as the ultimate. That is a tragedy of staggering proportions.[1]

Ezekiel 8:2–3 says, "I looked, and I saw a figure like that of a man. From what appeared to be his waist down he was like fire, and from there up his appearance was as bright as glowing metal. He stretched out what looked like a hand and took me by the hair of my head." What must God do to realize our spiritual weakness and worldliness? For some of us prophets (even those who have formerly received and faithfully communicated much prophetic vision), God may have to take us by the hair on our heads and force us to look into his tear-filled eyes.

The prophet Ezekiel had been given the arduous task of proclaiming God's impending judgment on his people. If God wasn't upset before, he was now. It was bad enough that abominable practices were commonplace in the homes, streets, and marketplaces of Jerusalem. But now the temple itself was being defiled. Worse, few of the nation's religious leaders seemed upset about it. Thus, the angel of the Lord was sent to find and mark the few who recognized the sordid state of the temple and grieved for it, so that they would be spared. The rest of the people would be slaughtered. Even more poignant is this: God's judgment was to begin with the Jewish elders in front of the temple itself.

Lay leaders, pastors, church leaders at all levels, must we too be taken "by the hair of our heads" in order to see our condition? Would the angel of the Lord mark us as people who lament the spiritual state of our nation? Or would God's judgment begin with us because we are condemned by our complacent comfort, our "ease in Zion" (Amos 6:1 KJV)?

---

1. A. W. Tozer, *Tozer on the Holy Spirit: A 366 Day Devotional*, compiled by Marilynne E. Foster (Camp Hill, PA: Christian Publications, 2000). From the July 27 devotional titled "Pleasures and Treasures."

In my heart of hearts, I believe you share this burden with me and with many others who have come before us. I believe we are ready to begin a renewed process of temple cleansing. Only then will the glory of the Lord be free to return to our midst in all of his power and splendor.

All is not doom and gloom. Doom was not the last word that Ezekiel received from the Lord. God promised that, as they heeded his warnings, "I will give them an undivided heart and put a new spirit in them; I will remove from them their heart of stone and give them a new heart of flesh. Then they will follow my decrees and be careful to keep my laws. They will be my people, and I will be their God" (Eze 11:19–20). That can be our promise as well.

One Church of God hymn writer expressed our heart cry in this way:

> Lord, I would be wholly Thine,
> I would do Thy will divine,
> From the world and sin and self I would be free.
> On the altar now I lie,
> And with all my heart I cry,
> Let the holy fire from heaven fall on me.
>
> Let the fire fall on me.
> Let the fire fall on me.
> The fire of Pentecost,
> Consuming sin and dross,
> Let the holy fire from heaven fall on me.[2]

Let this not only be the anthem we sing but the life we lead in every sacrificial, miraculously "normal" way!

---

2. William J. Henry, "Let the Fire Fall on Me," in *Worship the Lord: Hymnal of the Church of God* (Anderson, IN: Warner Press, 1989), 483.

17.

What's Right
with the Church of God?

*I tell you the truth, if you have faith as small as a mustard seed,
you can say to this mountain, "Move from here to there" and
it will move. Nothing will be impossible for you. —Matthew
17:20–21*

I remember thinking as a young child that the Church of God reformation movement must be the whole world! It was certainly our family's world; all of life seemed to revolve around the church. Only when I attended Dayton Christian High School did I begin to realize that there were actually other groups of wonderful people who loved Jesus—and some of those groups were bigger than the Church of God! (I recall being uncomfortable with this new idea! How could there be anything bigger than Springfield Camp Meeting or Anderson Camp Meeting? Where were there any bigger names in Christian music than Ron and Carolyn Patty or Bill and Gloria Gaither? After all, everywhere we traveled in the summers with our choir and work camp tours, there was the Church of God!)

To be sure, I am thankful for parents who established my world view as thoroughly Christian, seen through the lens of the Church of God reformation movement. You couldn't have convinced me that there was anything better!

I believe this still today. Of course, I know the statistics as well as you do. Our movement is dwarfed numerically and in scope of global influence by other Christian movements, as well as by the mainline denominations. But I still believe that the Church of God movement is a vital part of what the Spirit of God is doing in these last days! Just what part is that? Let me cast a vision for you.

It was time for Pastor Bob Hunt (our worship arts pastor) to share the devotional thought in our staff meeting. He shared from Matthew 2, focusing on verse 12: "And having been warned in a dream not to go back to Herod, they returned to their country by another route." Pastor Bob commented that, because of their personal experience with Jesus and a dream given to them by God, these men were changed. They left the scene as different men and they could not help but go a different direction—spiritually, emotionally, and physically—than they had traveled before! He concluded with a thought concerning our own ministry. "Are we willing to be changed and to go a different way as the Spirit leads?" he asked.

Pastor Bob reminded us that there are three basic types of people in our world: those who make things happen, those who watch things happen, and those who ask, "What happened?" The challenge for us as ministry leaders is to heed the dreams God has given us and be willing to make things happen, even if it means blazing a new trail and going by a different route than we have used before.

Consider the challenge against a business-as-usual, tradition-bound mentality posed by A. L. Byers, "Any tendency to establish traditions, or to regard a past course as giving direction in all respects for the future, or to become self-centered and manifest a 'we are it' spirit and bar the door of progress against the entrance of further light and truth, or in any way to refuse fellowship with any others who may be Christians, would itself be sectarian, altogether unlike the true reformation, which, if it be final, must necessarily be a restoration and possess universal characteristics."[1] This spirit is what was and is so right about the Church of God.

Which type of people are we? As a movement, we have always been willing to step out on faith as the Spirit of God leads, however innovative, ground-breaking, norm-busting, or absolutely unpopular it may be. We have always been willing, by the grace and power of God, to make things happen. And why not? We have been given the clearest message

---

1. Andrew L. Byers, *Birth of a Reformation: Life and Labors of Daniel S. Warner* (Anderson, IN: Gospel Trumpet Co., 1921), 32.

and the greatest commissioned authority. We have been prepared and positioned historically. And we are motivated to act boldly as we look to the precious promise of the imminent second coming of our Lord and Savior, Jesus Christ.

Then forward let us go,
Our hearts with love aflame,
Our snowy banner borne aloft,
Inscribed with Jesus' name.
The hosts of evil flee,
And heaven's open gates
Invite me now to enter where
Eternal glory waits.

I'm going on, I'm going on,
Until the final triumph, I'm going on.
I'm going on, I'm going on.
Until the final triumph, I'm going on![2]

2. Charles W. Naylor, "I'm Going On," in *Worship the Lord: Hymnal of the Church of God* (Anderson, IN: Warner Press, 1989), 685.

Appendix

Covenant Ministry in the History of the Church of God Reformation Movement

(From *Birth of a Reformation: The Life and Labors of Daniel S. Warner*, by A.L. Byers. Reprinted by permission of Faith Publishing House.)

O N THE 19TH he took the train on his journey toward Canton. He stopped at Loudonville and visited the church. Arrived at Canton on the 20th and proceeded immediately to visit congregations on the circuit. Sister Warner and child arrived on the 23d. The search for a house in which to live extended over a period of several days. There were good, faithful brethren who assisted them with provisions, but yet to a considerable extent they were left to provide the necessaries of life themselves. Of his effort to procure wood and hay we observe, for November 6:

> Cold. Snowed some last night for the first. Went to hunt wood and hay. Found no wood or hay to spare. It seems hard that a poor messenger of God must expose himself to drive about sixteen miles through mud and very raw air to hunt those necessaries. It seems a light thing nowadays to sow to the people spiritual things, but a heavy thing to reap a few temporal things, even when we try to live more simple and cheap than our poor. Oh, how good it would have been for me to have had this day in the warm with the Lord in my library! But glory to Jesus, we still joy in sustaining sacrifice for his sake and feel content with our lot. Only, dear Lord, give us a good supply of the spirit of love, zeal, wisdom, and power.

Meetings in town were held from house to house until a permanent place of worship could be opened. It was not long, however, until they both felt the Lord leading them to resign the circuit. Brother Warner had accepted with submission and good grace the charge given him (which, after all, was of man's appointment), but as a preacher of holiness with an ever increasing interest in a wider field, he doubtless felt that God wanted him to be free to go and do as the Spirit directed. The following is his entry for November 23:

> This morn before daylight, when having morning devotion, the Spirit of God spoke to both Sarah and me to fast today. Thank God for such a precious Leader. Who would not obey such a wise Counselor? Spent most of the day in reading the Word, singing, and prayer. At ten A.M. we were both before the Lord in silent prayer when we were both directed by the Spirit to resign this circuit. Still on our knees, we made known the orders received. We could but say amen and the refreshing from the presence of the Lord came upon our hungry souls. We engaged in prayer and praise when I was directed to proceed at once to write my resignation.

> This tried me, as I had never before been thrown among such very kind brethren and sisters. It seemed hard that I must throw up the circuit without as much as consulting them. But we dared not disobey God, as some hesitancy to obey in the past had cost me much power and sweet rest in God. Praise God. Our hearts were much lightened and we felt that we had now got back at the beginning of the highway of holiness which we had to some extent missed. We could now sing, "He leadeth us." Eve., went up to the office and received a card earnestly calling for our services at Columbiana. Of this call I had an impression before I went to the office, and believe it of the Lord. Glory to God! My way has been hedged up ever since we came on the circuit.

At Columbiana he found a number whose hearts were open to sanctification. His work there resulted in ten persons receiving the experience and one sinner being converted. Returning to his house in Canton on December 6, he became impressed with the idea of writing out in somewhat itemized form the solemn covenant that constituted his consecration to God.

8. I fasted today. Remained up with the Lord until after 11 o'clock at night. I was led by the Spirit to a deep self-examination. I found myself utterly nothing in the sight of God. I read with great interest the experience of Bro. R. Yeakel, in the Living Epistles of 1873. As I read over the solemn written covenant that this holy man entered into with God, I was much impressed to do likewise, but feared that my impressions came from a wish to imitate one of God's holy men rather than to follow the Spirit.

Went to the office this eve and received a letter from Brother Chambers, chairman of the Ohio Holiness Alliance. As soon as I saw his name on the envelope the conviction of last Sabbath that I should give myself up to be a holiness evangelist came strongly to my mind, and as I walked home I promised God that I would not lie down until I had reported myself to Brother Chambers for this work. The Lord helped me to do so, and as I wrote down my convictions and surrendered to the Lord, the Holy Ghost graciously fell upon my soul.

13. The day was mild and fair. Took a walk in the woods to commune with God. Thought much of the words of God, "I will make a new covenant with the house of Israel" (Jer.31:31). In Hebrews 8 and 10 I read that this covenant related to the new dispensation, and the apostle, in Hebrews 10, actually connects it with sanctification. I felt like entering more personally and formally into this covenant with the Almighty. But I thought, Can such a worm enter into an ev-

erlasting covenant with the Holy God of the universe? God makes the proposition, and with solemn reverence I venture to step out upon it. And this I do in the name of the Lord Jesus, my only righteousness.

A covenant is an agreement of two parties in which both voluntarily bind themselves to fill certain conditions and receive certain benefits. God is the party of the first part of the contract, and has bound himself,

1. "I will put my laws into their minds and write them in their hearts."

2. "And I will be their God."

3. They "shall know me from the least to the greatest."

4. "I will be merciful to their unrighteousness."

5. "Their sins and their iniquities will I remember no more."

O thou Most High God, thou hast left this covenant in thy Holy Book, saying, "If any man will take hold of my covenant." Now, therefore, in holy fear and reverence, I present myself as the party of the second part and subscribe my name to the holy article of agreement, and following thy example will here and now write down the conditions on my part.

"They shall be my people." Jer. 31:33. Amen, Lord, I am forever thine.

The vow is passed beyond repeal,

Now will I set the solemn seal.

Lord, thou hast been true to thy covenant, though I have been most unfaithful and am now altogether unworthy to take hold of thy most gracious covenant. But knowing that thou hast bound thyself in thy own free offer to "be merciful to their unrighteousness," I take courage to approach thee and would most earnestly beseech thee to fulfill thy wonderful offer to BE MY GOD and I do most joyfully yield myself entirely TO BE THINE.

Therefore this soul which thou hast made in thine own image is placed wholly in thy hands to do with it as seemeth good.

This mind shall think only for thy glory and the promotion of thy cause.

This will is thy will, O God!

The spirit within this body is now thine; do with it as thou wilt in life and death.

This body is thy temple forevermore.

These hands shall work only for thee.

These eyes to see thy adorable works and thy holy law.

This tongue and these lips to speak only holiness unto the Lord.

These ears to hear thy voice alone.

These feet to walk only in thy ways.

And all my being is now and forever thine.

In signing my name to this solemn covenant I am aware that I bind myself to live, act, speak, think, move, sit, stand up, lie down, eat, drink, hear, see, feel, and whatsoever I do all the days and nights of my life to do all continually and exclusively to the glory of God. I must henceforth wear nothing but what honors God. I must have nothing in my possession or under my control but such as I can consistently write upon, "Holiness unto the Lord" The place where I live must be wholly dedicated to God. Every item of goods or property that is under my control is hereby conveyed fully over into the hands of God to be used by Him as He will and to be taken from my stewardship whenever the great Owner wishes, and it is not my business at all.

She whom I call my wife belongs forevermore to God. Use her as thou wilt and where thou wilt and leave her with me or take her from me, just as seemeth good to thee and to thy glory. Amen.

Levilla Modest, whom we love as a dear child bestowed upon us by thy infinite goodness, is hereby returned to thee. If thou wilt leave us to care for her and teach her of her true Father and Owner, we will do the best we can by thy aid to make her profitable unto thee. But if thou deemest us unfit to properly rear or wouldst have her in thy more immediate presence, she is thine. Take her. Amen and amen.

And now, great and merciful Father, thou to whom I belong with all that pertains to me, and thou who art mine with all that pertains to thy fullness and richness, all this offering which made would be but foolishness and waste of time were it not for what I have in thee obtained to confirm the solemn contract. For were it not that thou art my God, my promises would be but idle words. I could fulfill nothing which my mouth has uttered and my pen has written. But since thou, Almighty, Omniscient, Omnipresent, and Eternal God, art mine, I have a thousand fold assurance that all shall be fulfilled through thy fullness.

My ignorance is fully supplied by thy own infinite wisdom. My utter weakness and inability to preserve myself from sin is abundantly supplied by thy omnipotence, to thy everlasting praise.

Glory to thy holy name! Though I have solemnly pledged all things to thee, yet, as thou art my "all and in all," I have to fear. Now, O Father! my God and Savior. I humbly pray thee so to keep me that all my powers of soul, body, and spirit, my time, talents, will, influence, words, and works shall continually, exclusively, and eternally glorify thy holy name through Jesus Christ, my Lord and Savior. Amen and amen.

In covenant with the God of all grace and mercy, who has become my salvation, my all, and whose I am forever, to the praise of His glory. Amen.

Entered into by the direction of the Holy Spirit and signed this thirteenth day of December, in the year of our Lord Eighteen Hundred and Seventy-Seven.

DANIEL SIDNEY WARNER

I realized much strength by obeying the impressions of the Spirit in writing out the foregoing covenant. God seemed present as though I was making an agreement with a person whom I could see by my side.